A Good Time TO LIVE

AN AUTOBIOGRAPHY OF LIFE
IN THE LATE 20TH CENTURY

BRUCE R. KINDIG

Copyright © 2023 Bruce R. Kindig

All rights reserved. No part of this book may be reproduced, stored, or transmitted by any means—whether auditory, graphic, mechanical, or electronic—without written permission of both publisher and author, except in the case of brief excerpts used in critical articles and reviews. Unauthorized reproduction of any part of this work is illegal and is punishable by law.

ISBN: 979-8-88640-959-8 (sc)
ISBN: 979-8-88640-960-4 (hc)
ISBN: 979-8-88640-961-1 (e)

Because of the dynamic nature of the Internet, any web addresses or links contained in this book may have changed since publication and may no longer be valid. The views expressed in this work are solely those of the author and do not necessarily reflect the views of the publisher, and the publisher hereby disclaims any responsibility for them.

One Galleria Blvd., Suite 1900, Metairie, LA 70001
1-888-421-2397

CONTENTS

Introduction v

Chapter 1 19th Century Ancestry... 1
           The family foundation

Chapter 2 Early Twentieth Century 7
           American Roots

Chapter 3 The 1950's 17
           Growing Up in Midwest America

Chapter 4 The 1960's 27
           My awakening to the World

Chapter 5 The 1970's 43
           Building a Family and Career

Chapter 6 The 1980's 59
           The Reagan Dividend

Chapter 7 The 1990's 75
           Pursuit of Goals

Chapter 8 The 2000's.. 89
           Toward Retirement

Epilogue: Beyond 2010... 99
           Retirement

INTRODUCTION

This book tells my life story about growing up in the Midwest of North America. Although it is written as an autobiography the theme of the book represents what I consider a very good time to be alive on planet earth. Any person could describe their time on earth as the best time to live. However, by the mid-twentieth century many diseases had come under control through various medicines and through a strong sense of hygiene. The comforts of modern living were taken for granted by my generation. We had indoor plumbing, flush toilets, electricity and natural gas furnaces to keep warm in the winter. Although air conditioning was available it would not become commonplace in people's homes until the 1960's. When I was born most of the countries of Africa, Asia and Latin America were considered third world. This meant that the people living there did not have many of the conveniences of my world.

Generally, I grew up in a time of peace. Two great world wars had killed millions of people just prior to my birth. Great plagues had happened in the past including the great influenza outbreak in 1919 in North America and other places. Wars seem to be around frequently and they existed during my lifetime. Many people have suffered or are still suffering from the effects of disease, war and famine. However, the North American continent has not seen bloody battles or invasions of its soil for well over a hundred years. One attribute of my life is that I did not have to deal with death, starvation or plague except in a few cases. I never missed a day of school, including college, after the 7th grade. I missed so few days of work from sickness that they will be mentioned in this book. At the writing of this book I have never been a patient in a hospital except one day for a kidney stone.

I would not consider myself wealthy although I lived in a good economic time. I had a lot of economic affluence. Take a look at the New York Stock Exchange from 1950 to 2000, you will see a steady increase in economic wealth. This wealth continued to expand into the 21st century. One does not have to actually own stock to receive the benefits of a vibrant economy. Rich people have always had more comforts than everyone else merely because they had money and could buy whatever they wanted. The title of this book is my story. Some would say that I had affluence and others would use the modern term, white privilege. Where I grew up there were few minorities. That I didn't have much contact with minorities early in my life was merely an accident of the time that I lived. I assure you that I was not born into wealth and that my ancestors had to work for everything they had. I have included in this book figures about my income and expenses for reference to history. Living in the United States meant that I had opportunity. Opportunity only works for someone who will take a chance at education or work. I took chances but usually had the odds with me as I often calculated the effects of the choices I made in life. I also took risks and enjoyed being with risk takers. I'm not talking about daredevil risks but risks of sport and life. The term, which would describe my family, is self-reliant. The ability to improve one's own life by taking the risk offered at every opportunity that comes along is a life skill. Life is a series of choices. If someone chooses to get drunk and tries to drive home, but he or she is killed in a car crash, that is the result of a bad choice.

This book will focus on the years 1950 to 2000. We will spend some time in the nineteenth century where my life took roots in my ancestors. We will look at how their background and upbringing forged my family and how they came to live in the Midwest, actually Iowa. We will examine life in the early twentieth century and even into the first two decades of the twenty-first century.

CHAPTER 1

19th Century Ancestry

The family foundation

My paternal great-great grandfather, Dominic Kindig, was born in Regensburg, Bavaria in 1819. Today Bavaria is in Germany but in those days a king ruled Bavaria. Munich was the capitol of Bavaria and Regensburg was about 88 miles (140 km) northeast of Munich. The 1820's and 1830's was a peaceful time in Bavaria. The wars against Napoleon had ended in 1815 and all of the German states were beginning to become more prosperous as the industrial revolution was flourishing in the German lands.

Little is known of Dominic and his occupation escapes us today. The revolutions of 1848 did not seem to affect Dominic, as there is no indication that he was political. He married Katrina Meyehover sometime around 1845 but it is in the family *Bible* that we see some details about his family. The family *Bible* is not really a *Bible* but a book of "*Epistles and Evangelism.*" It was published in 1843 in old German and features Bible readings and daily devotions of the Roman Catholic faith. The most important part is the first three pages of the book that contain hand written notes on family members. I received this book from my cousin Pat in 2011. While doing research on my family tree I discovered Pat on a search and contacted her. Having never been married and without children she mentioned how she had this book as well as a large picture of our great grandfather. Having no one to pass these items on to she sent them to me. I am truly grateful.

The "*Epistles and Devotions*" shows the names of twelve people born between 1846 and 1870. Caroline Kindig was born on 16 May 1846 but dies just two weeks later on 30 May. More children died in sequence: Maria 1847, Ludwig 1849, Anna 1850 and twins Johann and George 1857. Christina, born on 6 January 1855 was the first child to live to adulthood. Childbirth was a difficult experience in those days since no one went to the hospital to have a baby. We aren't sure of the circumstances of these deaths as some of the children lived only a few hours while others lived several weeks. To make it through childhood was a dangerous and difficult task. One other child, Jafasala died in 1865 after living only one hour. Along with Christina four other children would make it through childhood. They were Johann Baptist 1858, George Anton 1860, Afoa Katherine 1862 and Ludwig 1870. The three boys that lived carried the name of a brother who had died before them. The date of the deaths of Dominic and his wife Katrina were not recorded in the book.

My great grandfather George Anton Kindig was born on 12 June 1860 at 9:00 p.m. In Bavaria two major wars occurred in his childhood. The Austro-Prussian War was fought in 1866 when he was only six. Bavaria had sided with Austria in the war but after the war was forced to attach its allegiance to Prussia. When George was ten, the Franco-Prussian War was fought between various German states led by Prussia against France. France was defeated in this war. Bavaria would unite with all of the German States to create the new state of Germany. At no time did armies invade Bavaria during these wars and not much is known about Dominic's family during this time.

It was the custom in the 1870's that all able-bodied men must participate in compulsory military service. There was tension between France and Germany after the Germans had forced reparations upon the French and annexed Alsace-Lorraine at the conclusion of the Franco-Prussian War. So, George was drafted into the army in 1878 or 1879. My cousin Pat gave me a large portrait of George wearing his army uniform. It is in black and white but resembles the uniform of the Bavarian Army. Bavaria kept a separate army in those days but had to follow the policies of the German government. Conscription usually lasted two or three years and when George was discharged back to civilian society he must not have had an occupation to fall back upon because he was now interested in moving to America. Germany was a bustling country in the 1880's with hard work available at some of the large mining businesses or steel foundries. Whatever Dominic's job was, apparently it was not something one would inherit. And although there were opportunities to work in Germany its growing businesses could not absorb all of the growing population. Besides, George's older brother Johann had already immigrated to the United States and encouraged his brother to come and join him.

Johann came to the United States in 1874 at the age of sixteen. Here he changed his name to John. Not finding work he joined the U.S. Army by joining the 17th Infantry Regiment where he was a bugler. He was discharged in 1877 because of a disability. After his hitch in the army John traveled around for several years looking for work. He lived for a while in St. Louis and in northern Missouri. He lived in several towns in Iowa and Minnesota. In 1880, he married Lucy G. Hodge while living in Keokuk, Iowa. John persuaded George to come and live with him and in 1885 George came to the United States. At that time John lived in Ft. Madison, Iowa where he had a job as a guard at the Iowa State Penitentiary. George also got a job as a prison guard. A few years later John moved to Texas. John would continue to travel throughout his life while raising eight children. Eventually he settled in Bakersfield, California and died 15 June 1927. He is buried in the military cemetery in Bakersfield and his descendants still live in the Bakersfield area. In the meantime, George married Anna Hoffman in 1886. We will pick up the rest of his story in the next chapter.

My maternal great-great grandfather, Franz Josef Loos, was born on 17 April 1819 in Neudorf, Austria. Neudorf is about 50 miles east of Vienna. Family lore says he was an accountant but not much is known about him. He married Maria Anna Seifert and they had two sons who lived to adulthood, Franz Josef Loos (24 January 1862) and Frank Loos (19 February 1866). Any other children or the deaths of anyone else in this family, is unknown. Other children may have survived. My mother has told me of packages arriving at Christmas time from Loos family members until World War I ended any mail. Franz Josef Jr. is my maternal great grandfather and was always known as Josef. His brother Frank was always with him even as an adult as Frank was mentally handicapped. When Franz Josef Sr. and Maria Anna died is unknown. However, we do know that Josef and Frank had moved to Bohemia and settled in Bettelgrun.

Today Bohemia is part of Czechia. This was a German speaking area of the Austro-Hungarian Empire and Bettelgrun was close to the border with Saxony (Germany). Bettelgrun no longer exists and cannot be found on a map. Lead was discovered after World War II in the nearby hills and the Soviets mined very heavily all of the lead in the area virtually destroying the town. German speaking people were all ordered out of the area and where any Loos descendants might be today is unknown. At

Bettelgrun Josef married Maria Reichel. They had one son, Joseph Adolph Loos, born on 27 December 1880. This is my grandfather. Maria died either from the burdens of childbirth or a short time later. Josef married again to Anna Srovenal. They would have six children. Four were born in Bohemia (Emil 1893, Antonia 1895, William 1897, and Irma 1900) and two in the United States (Dorothy 1906 and Gertrude 1909). Josef immigrated to the United States in 1903.

Life was hard in the nineteen century. My ancestors were not farm workers but lived in towns or villages as laborers. The work must have been hard and the wages meager. They traveled a little to find work but generally settled down in one place. Getting through childhood was difficult. Several babies died from the harsh conditions. Wars did not seem to affect their lives but something encouraged these ancestors to give up this life style and move to America. Why did they take this risk? It is not recorded anywhere and no one seems to have spoken about it. It is difficult today to know the reason but I look at my own life for the answer. They were looking for an opportunity to live a better life. Life is full of choices and some choices involve risk. I have made some of these choices so I understand what they went through.

My ancestors were common people raising their families and working to feed them. No one was killed in a war or even a tragic accident. No one was robbed or raped and no one was sent to prison. Those who survived childhood remained healthy and we can assume long lives based on the longevity of their children. They were religious people of the Roman Catholic faith. Religion provides people with moral principles and a reason to live. It also encourages a vibrant family life. This would continue when they arrived in the United States and is one of the foundations of my life. They also did not seem to be very political either in Europe or after they arrived in America. Three factors seem to be the driving values of my family as they entered the twentieth century: family, religion and work.

CHAPTER 2

Early Twentieth Century

American Roots

George Anton Kindig came to the United States in 1885 at the age of 25. He lived with his brother John in Ft. Madison, Iowa where they both had jobs as prison guards. George had very little money when he arrived and apparently no vocation. He soon met twenty-year-old Anna Gabeline and they married in 1886. Anna had been born in Bavaria but not much more is known of her. George and Anna will have a family of seven children (Kate 1887, Alma Marie 1890, Bertha 1893, George William 1895, Louis William 1899, Margaret 1902 and Arnold 1905). Louis William Kindig is my grandfather. In 1904 George moved his family to Burlington, Iowa where he became the brew master at Moen Brewery.

Photos of George at the brewery show a somewhat short man with a large mustache. He seems to have always had a mustache from the photo in his army uniform to the photos taken just before his death in 1936. At the Moen Brewery, we see a happy man with his tankard of beer at the loading docks with his work mates. Burlington had a large German population and George was a member of the German Military Society. He was the vice-president of the society in 1914, which was the last year of the club. World War I had ended the club and soon prohibition would end the brewery.

In 1916 Iowa passed its own prohibition law that ended the making and selling of alcoholic beverages. The Moen Brewery closed in 1917 after trying to make soft drinks failed. George would go on to work at a local grocery store stocking shelves and carrying out groceries. His wife Anna died in 1920 at age 54. The cause of death is not recorded. Around this time George moved in with his oldest daughter Kate and her husband Benjamin Gillespie. With no social security in those days, family had to help each other. George worked when he could from the age of 60 until he died at the age of 76. He had come to the United States with almost no money; worked as a prison guard and a brew master and raised seven children. There were no childhood deaths and George's children stayed close together in Burlington. They attended church at the local Catholic parish and eventually owned property

Meanwhile, 41-year-old Josef Loos (Franz Josef Jr.) and his wife Anna came to America in 1903. They came with their three children on a ship named *Kimnitz*. Their son William died in 1899 at the age of 2. The ship docked at Baltimore where they lived for about a month. Josef had little money and several mouths to feed and was looking for work. He moved his family to Duquesne, Pennsylvania and then to Antigo, Wisconsin. By 1904 he finally settled in Oshkosh, Wisconsin where he settled permanently. Here he completed his family by having two more daughters. He worked at the local sawmill and was a member of Sacred Heart Catholic Church. The 1910 census shows two of his children also working to support the family. Emil, age 17 worked at the sawmill and Antonia, age 15 worked in a factory. Josef was very proud when he officially became a U.S. citizen in 1914.

Shortly after arriving in the United States, Josef wrote to Joseph Adolph Loos, his son from his first marriage, and asked him to bring his brother Frank to America. Joseph had recently married Johanna Schmidt in Bettelgrun and took the trip without her. He would send for her after he arrived in Oshkosh. Joseph and Frank traveled on the ship *Barbarossa*, arriving in New York on 9 June 1904. Johanna Loos (my grandmother, who went by the name Jenny) brought her mother (Johanna Schmidt) with her to New York on board the *Fredrich der Grosse* on 28 September 1904. Jenny was already pregnant with her first child.

Frank moved in with his brother Josef, as did Joseph and Jenny until they could get settled. Both Frank and Joseph went to work at a sawmill in Oshkosh. On 10 June 1916 Josef died from a heart attack. He was 54. Frank went to live with his nephew Joseph and at some time would live as a boarder with others. He worked odd jobs for the rest of his life with the 1920 census recording his occupation as ditch digger. My mother fondly remembers Uncle Frank as the man that lived above the garage. He died of a cerebral hemorrhage in 1956 at the age of 80. Josef's wife Anna would go on to marry a Mr. Schiessl. Anna died in 1949 at the age of 77. Her children stayed in Oshkosh except for Emil who moved to San Diego, California. So, the names Loos, Poeschl, Fink, Stockinger and Libowski are all related to my great grandfather Franz Josef Loos Jr.

My paternal grandfather, Louis Walter Kindig was born in Ft. Madison, Iowa on 20 September 1899. He was the fifth child of George and Anna Kindig. Louis, called Louie most of his life, graduated from high school as most of the Kindig children did. Although many people only went to school until the eighth grade in those days and some even less because school attendance was not required. We have seen already that children of the Loos family went to work as teen-agers; we do not have any early jobs known for Louis. His older brother, George Jr., had been an apprentice to a cabinetmaker and soon Louis also went to work there. Louis was a cabinetmaker until the depression came in the 1930's. Louis had a reputation as a lady's man but Sarah Marie Fetzer is the lady that brought him to the alter.

Sarah Marie Fetzer, my grandmother, was born in 1899 in Burlington. She apparently had an older sister that died during childbirth. She had two brothers and two sisters. Her father, George A. Fetzer, was born in 1872 in Iowa but her grandfather Frederick Fetzer was born in 1846 in Wurttemberg (Germany). Frederick had married Maria Pistorius from Prussia. Sarah also had ancestors from Mecklenburg. I only mention this because from her background she was raised a Lutheran and she married Louis Kindig, who was Roman Catholic. In those days, Roman Catholics could not marry a protestant and Sarah was not about to become Catholic. So, Louis changed his religion to Lutheran when they were married in 1921. My protestant upbringing is a result of this change in religion of Louis Kindig.

Louis and Sarah had two children, Robert Louis (1923) and Wilma (1925). Robert Louis Kindig is my father. My father grew up in a small nuclear family. My grandfather, Louis had a full-time job as a cabinetmaker and my grandmother had given up a job teaching in a one-room schoolhouse to marry him. The 1920's were a good time to start a family as America was having a booming economy. They bought a small two-bedroom house at 1230 Stowe St. in Burlington. They owned a model-T Ford and engaged in typical family entertainment. Louis stayed close to his brothers and sisters as they got together frequently to play cards. Pinochle was a favorite and I still remember playing the game with family when Sarah was in her early seventies. During this time Louis and his brothers sang barbershop music. He was in a quartet well into the 1950's. There was no television in those days and even radio was in its infancy so playing games and singing with family was a good past time. This also showed that my grandfather worked a forty-hour workweek before there was a law about it.

Louis and Sarah Kindig experienced the Great Depression of the 1930's. My grandmother once told me of the insurance man that would come to the house once a week to collect a dime. Also, the hobos would come to the house occasionally. She would give them some soup or perhaps a nickel. Times were rough and eventually Louis lost his job working at N. W. Cabinet Co. Since work was hard to find in Burlington they made a trip to Oshkosh, Wisconsin because the lumber industry there was looking for skilled workers. Sarah's brother Clarence Fetzer, he was known as Babe, told them of the jobs there. So, they moved there but must have rented out their house since they moved back to it during World War II. During the war Louis took a job at a soap factory in Burlington where he worked until 1960 when the soap factory went out of business. My father found Louis a job in Cedar Falls, Iowa as a school custodian. Louis worked there for five years when he could retire at the age of sixty-five and collect social security. Louis and Sarah returned to their only home they ever owned and retired in 1965. Louis died of cancer in November 1972. He had been a heavy smoker and also chewed tobacco. He was 73. Sarah died in May 1975 after a long bought with Alzheimer's disease. She was 76.

My paternal grandparents, Louis and Sarah Kindig, were strong in their Lutheran faith. When living in Burlington they belonged to Bethany Lutheran Church. When Bethany built a brand-new building near Crapo Park in the late 1950's, my grandfather installed the cabinets. They worked hard and raised two children instilling in them the importance of the Christian faith as well as the value of work. They owned property and I still remember that brand new 1958 Buick they had. They also enjoyed family leisure time, something probably unheard of in previous generations. They played cards and games or sang together in the evenings before the advent of television.

My maternal grandfather, Joseph Adolph Loos, lived in Oshkosh, Wisconsin from 1904 until his death in 1966. He and his wife Johanna had a total of eighteen children, but only eight lived to adulthood. Joseph Jr. was born 18 November 1904 but died of "macasmus" on 13 January

1905. Followed by Emma 1906 (died of brain injury), Elizabeth 1908 (died in a fire in 1920), Anna 1910 (born premature and died of convulsions), Ida 1911, Christine 1912, unnamed baby 1913, Carl Joseph 1915, Emil George 1917, Esther 1919, Irma Hedwig 1920, Arthur 1922 (died in 1927-described as a mercy killing by the family doctor), Richard Frederick 1923 and Theresa Mary 1926. Theresa Mary Loos is my mother. Four other births were stillborn or premature deaths and they were unnamed. A family this large required both parents to work. Elizabeth's death was a result of this situation. She was twelve years old and taking care of five younger siblings when her clothes caught on fire from cooking on the stove. Arthur's death, according to my grandmother who told my mother, was a doctor-administrated injection. Arthur was apparently mentally handicapped and ill. This type of euthanasia was apparently common in the 1920's.

My grandfather, Joseph Loos, took a job as a sander at one of the furniture factories in Oshkosh. Later he would work as a machinist and a finisher at Banderob and Chase Manufacturing Co. According to the 1905 Wisconsin State Census, my grandmother, Jenny, worked at Morgan Co. In the 1930's she worked as a housekeeper for some wealthy family. My mother remembers this because she cleaned the home while her mother did it for wages. My grandfather also was a bootlegger during prohibition. My mother remembers a G-man raid at her house but apparently no one was arrested. Sometime in the late 1930's Joseph Loos built a building next to his house at 4th and Ohio St. Here he started a hardware store and also used an outcropped building as a sheet metal shop. He ran this business until 1945. My mother remembers having to work there during World War II as the older siblings were married and had moved on. Her brother Richard was in the marines during the war so in 1945 when he returned he took over the business. Later the business was divided between Richard; he took the sheet metal shop, and his brother Emil, who ran the hardware store.

Joseph Adolph Loos retired in 1945 probably to avoid some business debts. He was sixty-five and lived the rest of his life in the family home and on social security. He later rented out the bottom floor of the house for some income. In retirement, he lost both of his legs to diabetes and I remember some family reunions with him in his wheelchair. He died in 1966 at the age of 86, probably from the diabetes. His wife Jenny had already died in 1944 of a heart attack.

My maternal grandparents were hard working people. They came to America with the shirts on their back. They raised a large family and everyone had to work to make ends meet. They were strong Roman Catholics and members of Sacred Heart parish in Oshkosh. This strong religious background and the willingness to work to get ahead are part of my family. Although they rented for some twenty years they eventually owned a house on Ohio St. Then they went into business for themselves. Like Louis Kindig and his siblings, the Joseph Loos children stuck together. Helping each other and keeping close contact they have instilled the strong sense of family. These strong German traits of work, family and religious faith are a big part of background.

My father, Robert Louis Kindig, was born on 15 June 1923 in Burlington, Iowa. His preteen and teenage years were during the depression of the 1930's. I know that he had some toys from the 1920's but I have never seen many of them. What I have seen, and now have in my possession are some of his marbles and two lead soldiers. Some of the marbles were homemade, made of clay, but others look like marbles of today. The two soldiers are about two and a half inches tall and hand painted. Much of the paint is worn off. There was a pickle factory near his home that used glass bottle stoppers. I remember playing with them as a small child just as he must have done, but they are no longer around. Around 1937 he moved with his family to Oshkosh. Clarence Fetzer had moved there from Burlington and found work at a furniture factory. His sister Laura Long (she married Paul Long) also lived there. Laura's daughter was Marge Long, my father's cousin, and her best friend was Theresa Loos. This is how my mother and father met. They were high school sweethearts.

My father graduated from Oshkosh High School in 1941 and went to work at a furniture factory. When the Japanese attacked Pearl Harbor, Hawaii on 7 December 1941 it was only a matter of time before my father would go to war. He enlisted in the army in early 1942 and went to boot camp. He was trained to be a ranger and did some training in Scotland.

Then shipped out to North Africa but did not see combat as the Germans retreated to Tunisia, later to surrender. He may have participated in the actions at Sicily but it must have been uneventful. In February 1943, the rangers were part of the invasion force at Anzio. Here the allies hoped to get behind the Germans in Italy and capture Rome. He was in the rear of a Higgins Boat (landing craft) approaching the beach when the boat was hit by a stuka or artillery. He had just climbed up the side and was about to jump into the water when the explosion threw him back into the boat. Nearly everyone was killed. He was wounded in the left arm and in the stomach. He was in the hospital on the beach when it was determined that his injuries were fatal, so he was moved to a separate part of the tent to die. Several hours later he was still alive so the surgeons decided to operate. They amputated his left arm. His stomach would eventually heal but it would cause him much grief for the rest of his life. Eventually he returned to the United States and was sent to a military hospital near Detroit. My mother took the train to see him several times. In late 1944 Robert Kindig was discharged from the hospital. He came home to Oshkosh wearing a uniform that I still have in my possession. The name inside the coat is not his. My mother and father were married in April 1945.

Theresa Mary Loos was born on 28 August 1926 in Oshkosh. As the last child of eighteen children she grew up in a house that was continuously getting smaller. She participated in dance groups and played on softball teams. Some of her childhood belongings I remember as a child was a Hawaiian guitar, her very flat softball glove and two large porcelain dolls. I still have the dolls and my mother gave me all of her dance costumes a few years ago. She graduated from Oshkosh High School in 1944, the same year her mother died. With the war going on she worked in her father's hardware store, sometimes having to drive a truck to Milwaukee to pick up things for the store. My mother and father decided to get married soon after, but what kind of work could a one-armed man do? My father decided to take advantage of the G.I. Bill and become a teacher, so they moved to Cedar Falls, Iowa to attend Iowa State Teachers College.

My parents lived in a Quonset hut on the school campus for about three years. My brother, Gregory James Kindig was born in 1946. My father, who admits he had never been a very good student, graduated early in December 1948. He was able to get a job as a teacher in the Cedar Falls Community School District and was assigned to Cedar Heights Elementary School. This was a K-8 school and he taught social studies in 7th and 8th grades. My parents were renting a house in North Cedar that did not have running water and the outhouse was in the back yard. The wash buckets that they used as a bathtub are still in my family. When my mother was pregnant with me, my parents participated in a program to win a few baby gifts. A new movie was coming out called "Apartment for Peggy." The local Regent Theater promoted my parents as the veteran and his pregnant wife searching for a place to live. Stories were written in the newspaper and a special event took place at the theater and I was going to be named Peggy. I was born on 6 April 1949 and named Bruce Robert Kindig.

My great grand parents took a risk when they decided to leave their homeland and come to the United States. Both George Kindig and Josef Loos had no skills and very little money. They took work when they found it and settled in one place for most of the rest of their lives. My grandparents are the first of my family to own property buying a home that they would live in until they died. Decisions had to be made that brought about some prosperity. Louis Kindig became a skilled cabinetmaker and Joseph Loos went into business for himself. Louis took a risk to move to Oshkosh during the depression, which led to my mother and father meeting, but returned to his home in Burlington once work was available there. My grandparents raised their children in their religious faith and they all received a good education. Although German was spoken by George Kindig and Joseph Loos all of their children learned English. Speaking English and getting a high school education made my ancestors Americans. My father joined the army in 1942 to fight against his ancestor's homeland. There is no doubt about the patriotism of my family. After the war, the G.I. Bill offered my father an opportunity as a veteran. My mother and father were married with almost no money and no skills. Going to college was a risk, but it seems like my ancestors took advantage of opportunities, worked hard at succeeding in these opportunities and generally were successful. My grandparents retired with only social security but lived in the house they owned. My great grandfathers never retired, but worked until they died.

Living in the United States of America definitely is a place of opportunity. Had my ancestors stayed in Germany, this story might have ended here with much suffering. If they had moved to Africa, Asia or Latin America, over time they would have been less productive. My family remained healthy except for some of the children who didn't make it through childhood. It was not uncommon to live into one's 70's and 80's. Family background has allowed my family to be free from criminal activity, except maybe the bootleg still of Joseph Loos during prohibition. My ancestors were not political, although they did participate in elections. They worked hard, raised their family and became a little more prosperous than the generation before them. I entered this world at the beginning of the second half of the twentieth century. How would I handle the opportunities that lay ahead? Life is full of choices. In the previous chapters I only generalized about the choices my ancestors made. Now we will see the choices that I make. If I make the right choices I can say, "This is a good time to live."

One more thing; unless you are born rich, everyone starts out with nothing. To know poverty is a humbling experience. To be humble is a good character trait. The opportunities to improve yourself and the experiences from humble beginnings can make for a good life. As a fourth-generation immigrant to the United States we will now begin my story.

CHAPTER 3

The 1950's

Growing Up in Midwest America

The reader should understand the surroundings of life in the United States after World War II. The United States went on to have a booming economic development. The first twenty-five years of this boom provided everyone with jobs and the opportunities for increased wages. My parents may not have understood any of this at the time, nor was I aware of it either. I often thought my parents were poor but I think that was just how they acted as children of the depression. My parents never bought anything unless they had saved up the money for it first. My father always bought a car with cash. Only our home had a mortgage.

I am a member of the baby boom generation. This term didn't come about until much later but it was a time when married couples were having children. With the war over it was time to raise a family and it seemed like everyone was doing just that. My generation is the first generation to grow faster than any other generation. This was all attributed to childbirth and not immigration like previous generations. Because of this growth businesses were growing with the opportunity to sell new products and to a larger consumer group than ever before. First my generation needed baby products, then toys and clothes. As my generation aged it would lead to appliances, automobiles and housing. What a great time to be a child growing up.

In 1950, Cedar Falls, Iowa was a town of about 14,000 people. It was a college town with the Iowa State Teachers College on the southern part of town. There was very little industry in Cedar Falls but in Waterloo the John Deere Tractor Works and the Rath Packing Plant were big factories. Many people worked there and often lived in Cedar Falls, which was about 10 miles away. A trolley ran between the two towns and later a municipal transit bus would also provide a connection. There were no minorities in Cedar Falls. I grew up without any knowledge of life from another point of view. There was an African-American community in Waterloo but I rarely saw it.

When I was one year old my parents bought a house on the west side of Cedar Falls, just a mile from the Waterloo border. The house was a new story and a half with a basement and an unattached garage. It was built at 3422 Rownd St. in a new housing development. Rownd St. was named after the farmer who sold the land to the developers. It was a blacktop road with ditches on both sides of the street much like country roads. There were ten houses on the west side of the road that had a full acre of land. We lived on the seventh lot. Behind our house my father would cultivate a large garden. The house had all the latest conveniences such as running city water, plenty of electrical outlets and a natural gas furnace. Growing up I thought everyone had a house like this since every house in this neighborhood was like this. We were located just two blocks from US highway 218; that was the main road that connected Waterloo and Cedar Falls. My parents had a 20-year mortgage at four percent interest. The mortgage was for about $7500.

My father was a teacher in the Cedar Falls Community School District nine months of the year. He took a job as a security guard every summer at Chamberlin Manufacturing Company in Waterloo. He also developed his property into a large garden in which he sold the produce every summer. He had eight or ten trees in his orchard and grew cherries, pears and several kinds of apples. He was busy with strawberries and raspberries as well the usual vegetables of corn, snap beans, peas asparagus and rhubarb. My father would never consider himself to be handicapped because he only had one arm. In fact, he was always busy working at his jobs or working in his garden. He enjoyed hunting and fishing and often supplemented our groceries with fish, squirrel, pheasant and rabbit.

My mother did not have a job outside of the home. She raised my brother and me full time and took care of the house. She always canned the many vegetables from our garden and in our basement, we had a special "root cellar" area for all of the produce. She also made wine from the grapes that we grew. My mother drank the wine and also purchased beer from the store. However, I never saw my father ever drink any alcoholic beverage. Perhaps it was because of his scarred stomach from the war. Neither of my parents ever smoked and I don't recall seeing any of the other adults around me smoke either. Of all of my adult relatives only my grandfather, Louis, smoked cigarettes but never around us kids. My Uncle Richard smoked cigars. Smoking in the 1950's was supposedly the thing to do as it was heavily advertised and the connection of smoking with cancer was not well known.

My parents were members of St. John Lutheran Church since they moved to Cedar Falls in 1945. I was baptized here and my parents saw to it that I attended Sunday school. We would get an award for perfect attendance. It was a small pin that could be worn on your clothing. I recall having seven or eight years of perfect attendance before confirmation. In Sunday school, I had many friends. We were all baby boomers seeing new arrivals all of the time. In the summer, we had two weeks of Bible school. We had instruction and singing from 8:00 to 11:30 and always got out late. We had a thirty-minute recess where I always participated in the softball game with the older kids. We didn't play on teams, but rather played work-up. Imagine four batters against thirty to forty fielders. My parents had family devotions most evenings after supper. This is where I learned many of the Bible stories I still remember today. After we got a television the devotions happened less frequent. It seemed like everyone went to church in the 1950's.

My parents were firm believers of taking a family vacation. Every August we would take a one or two-week vacation somewhere. I have a vague memory of camping at Yellowstone Park when I was three. Often, we went to Minnesota where my father, my brother and I would go fishing. Sometimes my brother and I were catching fish faster than my father could take them off the hook for us. I remember very well the long vacation we took in 1957. We were gone almost three weeks and visited the historic sights of New England. I was eight but my mother told me to say that I was seven if anyone asked. Children seven and under got in for free at many places. I was a leader of the pack at the House of Seven Gables and at Plymouth Plantation. This was my first experience with historical places. We never stayed in a motel but always went to a campground.

I started kindergarten in 1954. My first school was Cedar Heights Elementary School. Since the school was over a mile away my mother got together with other mothers to form a car pool. Nobody owned more than one car in those days so when it was my mother's turn to drive she would have to take my father to work and pick him up afterwards. This car pool brought me closer to some long-lasting friends. Two houses north on my house was Kim Rhoades and two houses south was John Lueders. A few houses away were Donald Johnston and David Loy. Finally, Terry Meewes (pronounced mavis), who lived along highway 218, completed the car pool. I don't remember how six of us all rode together in a car but no seat belts were required in those days. My teacher was Miss Margaret. My father told me later that everyone called her Miss Margaret because her last name was so hard to pronounce. I remember having a rug to take a nap on and also that we got a milk break. We learned how to tie our shoes and learned to read from books about "Dick, Jane and Sally." I was in the morning kindergarten so we all went home for lunch.

The next year I still went to Cedar Heights School but they had built an additional expansion building that would house first and second grade. Now that I was six I would ride my bicycle to school. I had a twenty-four-inch standard bike. There were no bikes with gears yet. I had to cross highway 218 to get to school and we had crossing guards that held a stop sign on a long pole. Everyone rode bikes to school and we did not lock them. I never heard of anyone having a bike stolen. There was no fear of strangers or pedophiles. I had Miss Keminga in first grade but don't remember much. I carried my lunch in those days. I was a picky eater and had a miracle whip sandwich most days. In second grade, I had Mrs. Smith. She was a friend of my father. At recess, we played marbles. My father taught me a lot of rules and my friends and I played when it was nice. Here I had my first girlfriend, Martha Henderson. Not much to say here since I went to a different school the next year and never spoke to her again. One rule I knew very well was that if any marbles fell on the floor Mrs. Smith would keep them.

On 21 February 1955 my sister, Valerie Sue Kindig, was born. Before she arrived, my parents decided that the upstairs of the house should be finished and made into a bedroom for us boys. My brother and I had shared the eight by ten bedroom in the rear of the house and now we would have a large twelve by twenty-five-foot bedroom upstairs. My grandfather, Louis, would construct the cabinets upstairs with built in draws in the wall and a double desk under the southern exposure window. On hot summer nights, a fan would be placed in the window to blow out the hot air. We had the best room in the house as my parents often slept on the porch when it was hot. I was six years older than my sister and because of that we were never close as children. I was out of elementary school before she entered it and out of high school before she started junior high.

My brother, Gregory, and I didn't play together very often. Our interests were different. I preferred to play alone and he was often a pest to me. He would knock over things I built or disrupt what I was making. One Christmas, we both got the same present. It was a Lionel electric train and my father would build a wooden platform for us to permanently run the train in the basement. The track was a large oval with a figure eight in the middle. I still have this train today and my grandchildren now run it once in a while. Toys I liked back in the 1950's included Lincoln Logs, Tinker Toys and Skyline, a plastic skyscraper building kit. However, my favorite toy was a Davy Crockett Alamo Set. This was a very popular topic because of Walt Disney. Some of my friends had coonskin caps and plastic muskets. I also collected cars and army men from cereal boxes. I had a bowl of cold cereal every morning for breakfast. I got the cars from eating Krinkles, a rice crispy type cereal made by Post. I don't remember where I got the army men but I had over 50 of them. I also had lots of cowboys and Indians.

We got our first television in 1954. Before we had a TV, my parents would listen to various radio programs while I played with my toys. I remember going to a neighbor house to watch Howdy Dowdy before we had a TV. This was probably the biggest thing to change my young life. The whole family watched television every night. We only got three stations and we talked about the good shows the next day at school. Everyone watched about the same thing. Every day after school I would watch The Mickey Mouse Club and a few other shows before our family sat down together for supper. On Saturday mornings, the TV only showed cartoons and children programming. I was mesmerized and entertained through my early childhood.

In 1957 a new school, Orchard Hill Elementary, was completed just two blocks south from my house. It only went to 4th grade and Mrs.

Smith was the first principal. She asked me and Kim Rhoades to be the first crossing guards at the school. The school was on Rownd Street so there wasn't very much traffic. After a couple days, the 4th graders took over the school patrol. Since the school was so close to my house I would go home for lunch. I knew something about the American Civil War in 3rd grade because I played a game called "Yankees and Confederates." We played this at recess but I don't remember much about it except I always chose the Confederate side. This will come up later in my life. I enjoyed school and all of the other kids in my class. In 3rd grade I learned to write in cursive and in 4th grade I learned the multiplication tables. For spelling our teacher had us learn how to spell the name of a classmate every week with our regular words. I'll never forget that Penny McCullough wanted us all to learn how to spell Penelope. She was always Penny.

In 1959 Orchard Hill School completed another expansion so that 5th and 6th grades were now in this school. The lower grades were now two classes of each grade. My 5th grade was too big for one classroom but not big enough for two. So about twelve or fifteen members of my class were in a split 4th/5th classroom. The new addition had outside doors that opened right out into the playground. What a great school. This was a very happy time in my life.

There were no organized sports before the fifth grade in the 1950's. I didn't know much about sports but I was very active. I remember in 3rd grade when a teacher put a bar across a door for everyone to do pull ups. I did ten, the most in my class. I wasn't particularly strong, just scrawny. We often had organized races at school. I was very fast at the short distances, probably the fastest in my class. Over time as new students arrived every year I slowly lost being the fastest or the strongest. A favorite recess game we played was bombardment. It is also called battle ball or dodge ball. I liked this game of throwing a ball at someone. One rule we played was that when one side was down to five players the other side could advance forward beyond the half line. I interpreted this to mean the same for the side with just five players. If I had a ball or two I would rush the larger team and get behind them. Without a ball and with a partner I would tackle an opponent so my partner could hit them with a ball. There we no rules about this and I soon had a reputation of being aggressive in sports.

I took my first swimming lessons when I was in 2nd grade. My mother took me to the YMCA in Waterloo. The class was all boys and we took the lessons naked. No one had a swimming suit. I didn't do very well as I would take swimming lessons for the next several years. I now took them at the Cedar Falls community swimming pool. This pool was a very large pool. It had a sand bottom but concrete walls. A continuous flow of water came in the center of the pool through a fountain. This water had been used to cool the generators at the Cedar Falls Utilities. One area was closed off because of the large drains. I spent many summer afternoons there. I could swim for just ten cents. I would ride my bike the three miles to the pool and over time I would be swimming in the deep areas.

During my early childhood, I made many friends. We all had stay at home moms and in the summer, ran free. Like free ranging chickens, we were free ranging children. I was outdoors by 8:00 a.m. and home by dark. One rule was that you had to be home for supper and if your father called or whistled you had to go home. The other kids did the same. My bicycle was my means of transportation. I explored everywhere. I went with some friends down country roads stopping at small creeks. We called them crickets; which was slang for crick, also slang for creek. We threw rocks or poked sticks in the mud, caught tadpoles or just explored. By the time I was in 5th grade I rode my bike all the way to downtown Cedar Falls, about four miles away. There I could buy a phosphate for a nickel. At the corner of Rownd St. and highway 218 was the Snow Cap drive-in. Here I bought a root beer for a nickel or when my mother wanted to make root beer floats she would send me there to bring back a quart. Of course, I had no money, but a pop bottle was worth three cents and if I could find a couple bottles I could take them to the Landmark Grocery Store. The Landmark was right next to the Snow Cap. It used to be a one-room schoolhouse so it wasn't very big. There I could buy penny candy and by 5th grade I had an interest in baseball. Baseball cards were one cent each and that included the bubblegum. Or for five cents I could get a pack of ten cards with one piece of bubblegum.

I didn't play with Kim Rhoades much because he always had to do chores. His father walked with crutches because of polio. My father didn't ask me to do too many chores but I did have to mow the lawn starting when I was about ten. Our yard was so big that I usually took a couple days to do it so that I could play with my friends often. John Lueders and I played frequently and on rainy days we would play board games. He went with me the first time I went to Kenneth Nelson's house. He never went back and because he went to Catholic School we didn't do much after that. Don Johnston and I would play army. We would get our father's army coat and hat and play soldier. In 4th grade his father died of cirrhosis of the liver and he moved away. I would join up with him again in high school. Terry Meewes and David Loy, I would do things with every now and then. But the person I spent the most time with was Kenneth Nelson. I met him in 3rd grade and almost always went to his house. He lived about four blocks away and had a younger brother, Gregory. In the summer, I played with Greg and Kenny almost every day. Their father was an engineer for the Illinois Central Railroad and was gone from home many days in a row. Their mother also had a job so there were no parents at home during the day. They had an older sister, Barbara, who watched them, but she was often not home.

The reader may notice the attraction of going to the Nelson house. No supervision; but then there wasn't much in the 1950s. Greg and Kenny always stayed home. They didn't have bicycles. I still went places with my other friends. At the Nelson house, we did things I would not do at home. Here we would build things in the sandbox and then run the hose through it to make a flood. After a heavy rain, we would go build dams in the street to control the water. What I liked best was the vacant lot next to their house. Here we made a baseball diamond and kids from all around would come and play workup. One summer we built a house on stilts in their back yard. It was about four by six feet and was about seven feet off the ground. One-day Barbara's boyfriend threw a large brick in the wall of our "fort." So, we took it apart and carried all the wood to my house. What happened next will be in the next chapter. I eventually fell away from Greg and Kenny. Their parents got divorced and I never saw them in school. Greg moved with his mother to California and Kenny graduated from high school with me. Later he died in a single car crash at the age of twenty-seven.

In 1959 my parents bought a seventeen-foot Mallard travel trailer. From now on, no more resort cabins or tents for my family. We took a trip over Christmas break to Florida. In the days before interstate highways this was a three-day trip one way. We slept every night in the trailer and spent six days in Florida. Growing up in the 1950s for me was a lot of fun.

The reader may think that this is not an accurate picture of American life. I was not a minority who would have had a different experience. If I lived in the state of Mississippi this story would be different. Certainly, this is true. That is actually the point to make in this book. I grew up in a small Midwest town where everyone I grew up had the same experience. This was a good time and place to live.

Up to this point I didn't make many decisions in my life. My parents provided food, shelter and clothing and a loving environment and I had a strong Christian background. I knew the difference between right and wrong. I was free to move about my environment without fear of harm or robbery. I never locked my bicycle and it was always where I left it. As my parent's income increased we accumulated more possessions and I could always find a little money. My parents opened a bank account for me when I was five or six and I would put some money in my account from time to time. I got a very good education and every student in my classes was just like me. I don't ever remember anyone misbehaving in school or being sent to the principal's office. What would my parents or my classmates think if I misbehaved? That idea was important to me as well as everyone around me.

CHAPTER 4

The 1960's

My awakening to the World

On 10 May 1960, I went to bed early like I always do. My mother says I was a perfect child in regards to going to bed before being asked. My mother woke me up before midnight to ask me a question. Who were the kids that were with my brother earlier that day? I gave her a name and went back to sleep. The next day I did not go to school. My father had found my brother hanging in a neighbor's barn. He had his hands tied and the police determined that it was an accident. This family tragedy has never been satisfactorily explained to this day. I didn't go to school until after the funeral. My brother had a Waterloo Courier paper route and I now took it over.

With my brother's death, my family changed. As an eleven-year old I took on more responsibilities. I was now the oldest and continued doing chores like lawn mowing, but I was a little more active with picking crops in the garden. Now I also had to get the newspapers delivered by 5:30 p.m. every day and early mornings on Sunday. Also, I now had an income. I bought all the baseball cards I wanted, started a coin collection and put money in the bank. I used my brother's bicycle to deliver the papers because he had large baskets over his rear fender. When I went out for sports my father would deliver the papers for me. As the neighborhood grew, so did the paper route. I started with forty customers and when I quit the route three years later I had eighty-seven.

The summer of 1960 Greg, Kenny and I moved the wooden fort to my back yard. At the far back of our property was a very tall tree where my brother had built a tree house. It was more like a platform about 40 feet in the air. It had partially collapsed and we build our tree fort about 6 feet off the ground. Greg and Kenny didn't come to my house often. Usually I played at their house. Now with a tree fort I decided to expand it. David Loy and Mike Mead joined me in building an extension from the tree fort out into the yard. We built a four by six feet structure on stilts from lumber we got at a monuments company and from crates behind a furniture store. Later we would get wood from the discard piles at the construction sites for new homes. Sometimes Terry Meewes would come along and engage us in dirt clod fights. It was better to fight in the open than in the fort. I had some money from my paper route and we bought nails and painted the fort brown. The next year we enclosed the bottom and built a third story. I learned some carpenter skills over the years. In the summer of 1963 we decided to expand the fort and took out the entire south wall. That night a strong storm came and destroyed our fort. My father helped me move the wreckage to a large pile where we burned it.

I entered 6th grade in 1960. I now became acquainted with presidential politics as the Nixon-Kennedy election took place that fall. At school our class also watched every Mercury space launch live on TV. Social Studies became my favorite subject and I liked historical things the most. I also wanted to be the class president. My main competition was Vickie Lutz. We knew each other from church before she came to Orchard Hill. In the end, I won the presidency. However, we also competed to be the captain of the safety patrol. Sometimes I was captain and sometimes she was captain. Neither one of us cornered the position. She also competed with me in band. I had taken lessons on the coronet and she had too. This competition would last through our senior year in high school where I held the 4th chair and she held the 5th.

A new student in my 6th grade was Milo Mead. He always went by the name of Mike. He was a cousin of Dave Loy and the three of us hung out a lot. Mike and I soon developed a strong attachment to strategy board games. It started with Stratego and soon led to war games. I got an Avalon Hill game called D-Day. It may have been a little over our heads but we stuck with it. Soon we had more games. I would get Waterloo and he would get Afrika Korps. I would get Bismarck and he would get Stalingrad. Over the years we both acquired quite a collection of war games. We would have a sleepover and roll dice far into the night. The last time I saw him was in 1972 when we were both married and we got together to play a war game. I have not seen him since but I still am very involved in strategy games.

Although I enjoy games very much and learned to play cards from my mother I also discovered sports and got very involved. In Cedar Falls the Amvets Club ran the little league and the Lion's Club ran the older league. Both baseball leagues ran in the afternoon and parents never came to games. After my 6th grade the Amvets held their games at Orchard Hill School. That was convenient. However, after 7th grade the Lion's Club league was held at a college field about three miles away. I rode my bike there. I played 3rd base and then played 2nd base. I loved the competition of the team sport. I was just an average player but some players were really good. I made the sophomore baseball team in High School. David Loy and I were told to show up for our first game and wore our uniforms to the bus pickup. There a coach told us we were not going on the bus trip. We were both devastated and since Dave's parents gave us a ride to the field we had to walk home. This was my first but not last time I had a coach break my heart. I never did play in a single game that summer.

I went out for football in 7th grade. I was the left half back on our team. Most people don't know what a half back is today. I learned the plays and carried the ball but I was too small. I didn't play in 8th grade but I did in 9th grade. This time I was left tackle. I know a lot about football but I knew I couldn't play this competitively.

In 6th grade everyone wanted to play basketball. I asked my parents for a basketball and would shoot hoops with some of my friends. In 7th grade I went out for basketball and there were so many of us that we had to have two different practice times. This was a big mistake in my life. I was a lousy basketball player but I was a competitive sports fan. I had picked the wrong sport. I should have gone out for wrestling except that I had never heard of it before.

So, in 8th grade I went out for wrestling. I was small but wiry and that suited me fine. I didn't do much in 8th and 9th grade and only wrestled once in competition. In my sophomore year, I was on the wrestling team when Beets Dotson was the assistant coach. He was a national champion college wrestler and I learned a lot from him. The head coach was Keith Young who was also a national champion. Some of my teammates called me elastic man because I was so flexible. In all of my wrestling matches I was never pinned. In December of 1964 the Cedar Falls wrestling team had a home meet against East Waterloo. I was wrestling 112 pounds on the reserve team. Today that is called the junior varsity. The reserves always had to roll out the mat for the meet. After we had finished Coach Dotson pointed out that my name was on the varsity board. The varsity wrestler Jimmy Christiansen had not made weight and I was now the varsity starter.

I lost my first varsity match by a score of 4-0 but had my picture on the front page of the sports section of the Waterloo Courier. It wasn't really my picture, but that of my opponent- Paul Stinson- the defending state champion. Paul went on to win a third title. I went to the Waterloo Courier and still have that photo.

If you are a wrestling fan reading this book you understand how wrestling can get into your blood. Wrestling had not just gotten into my blood but I was about to have wrestling become a major part of my life, and it still is today. I didn't train much that sophomore year but wrestled on the varsity squad about half of the season. I won most of my reserve matches but lost most of my varsity matches. I went out for track after wrestling so I could stay in shape. My parents bought me a weight lifting set and I began working out in my basement. I would be ready for my junior year.

Who was the best wrestler in Iowa in 1965? Any wrestling fan knows that answer. It was Dan Gable. Dan Gable wrestled at West Waterloo High School. In 1965, he was an undefeated two-time state champion and would win his third title. Dan Gable wrestled at 112 pounds and so did I. However, the night we wrestled West Waterloo I was on the reserve team and Todd Rhoades was our varsity starter. Todd was Kim Rhoades younger brother. What would Dan Gable's backup wrestler be like? I wrestled a guy named Kuecker and I won that match. Todd wrestled Gable and I remember that match very well. Gable was beating Todd very handily when he put Todd to his back. In those days, the referee did not blow the whistle when there was a pin; he just slapped the mat. There was a lot of noise as you could imagine and the cheerleaders were right on the edge of the mat clapping and slapping in their cheer. Suddenly Dan Gable stood up and put out his hand for the closing handshake. He had heard the cheerleaders slap the mat and thought he had pinned poor Todd Rhoades. Todd immediately got up and realized the match was not over and took Gable down. The match didn't end well for Todd Rhoades but he survived the third period and he was not pinned by Dan Gable.

Later that season I challenged Todd Rhoades for the varsity position. I had wrestled him in practice many times and figured I could take him. Coach Dotson was the referee of our match and it was very close. In a flurry of action, I broke away from Todd, who was in the top position, as we crashed into the wall mats. Coach Dotson did not award me the escape and I was furious. The only time in my life that I ever argued with a coach was at that moment. Of course, I didn't win the argument and I lost the match by one point. Todd went on to be the 127-pound state champion in 1968. He died in a motorcycle accident in 2010.

My senior year was going to be my big year. I had trained in the off-season, lifted weights and attended summer wrestling practice. I had moved up to 120 pounds and Todd Rhoades had gone to 127. My good friend Dick Messerly was at 112 after being behind me several years. Only a few sophomores were at my weight and I easily dominated them. It was difficult to earn a varsity letter in wrestling and I did not have one. You have to earn it, so this was my year. I had the varsity 120-pound spot in the lineup and was having a modest beginning. I wrestled at Osage, Iowa and had a 2-2 tie with their wrestler. The next wrestling meet was a Christmas tournament on a Saturday. The night before the meet Coach Young informed me that I was being replaced by a sophomore; Kevin Kazinski. No reason was given. I was devastated. I could beat Kazinski like nothing and a coach had the power to just change the lineup on a whim. My whole life had been ruined. I had planned and worked hard for this position and now it was gone. No chance for a wrestle off, I was finished and heart broken. I did not quit but continued to come to practice every day. I could still pound on Kazinski if the coaches allowed me to, but I would never wrestle again. At the end of the season I got my varsity letter, but it was a gift not an award. I never took it out of the envelope. One thing was learned from this life experience. I would never act in any way that takes away from a person something they have worked to earn. I dislike coaches who act like dictators. I will meet these people later in my life. When I went to college I tried to get on the college team but I didn't try very hard and eventually gave up.

My childhood friend Kim Rhoades won his third wrestling state championship at 165-pounds in 1967. He went on to Iowa State to wrestle. My sports days were over and I was going to the University of Northern Iowa to work on a career. Little did I know how all of my sports experiences would influence my life. I was going to become a 3A Iowa wrestling coach. That story is later.

In academics, I was just an average student. In 7th grade we started to get letter grades but I always pride myself that I could get an A in something. In 7th grade I got A's in Physical Education. In 8th grade I got A's in Health. In 9th grade I got A's in American History to 1877. I finally found my niche. I loved history and prided myself in my memory work. I could memorize names, dates and places like nobody else. I memorized all the presidents in order, then all of the states and when they entered the Union in order. In 9th grade I entered the Daughters of the American Revolution history test. I wanted to be number one. I took fourth place. In the summer of 1964 my family went on vacation to Washington D.C. On the way, we stopped at Gettysburg and I gave my parents the battlefield tour. I enjoyed this vacation very much and spent a lot of time in the gallery of the House of Representative.

Where did I get all of this information? In 7th grade I took an interest in history looking at information about the Civil War Centennial. If I wanted to know more I would need to read more. By 8th grade I would read every night before I went to bed. I would continue this through my high school years. I could get paperback books for twenty-five or thirty-five cents and my parents would order them for me through the mail. During Lent that year we would stop at the public library after the Wednesday evening service. I say that I read every Civil War book in the public library that year, but I am sure that is an exaggeration.

In 1963, I was confirmed in the Lutheran Church. There were thirty-six people in my confirmation class and we all had to go to class every Saturday for three hours for three years. We always had to memorize some Bible verses. My ability to memorize really helped me. Just before we were confirmed we had to have a public examination. All of us confirmands were in front of the church as the pastor asked each of us several questions. We had to give an answer and give a Bible verse. This was very hard compared to what people go through today.

My high school years were very busy. I spent a lot of time on sports, particularly wrestling. I was in the marching band and played some duets with my friend Mike Mead. He and I continued to play war games and I even started to play the games by mail with adults. I won the vast majority of the games. I read books every night before I went to sleep and always carried a paperback to study hall. My grades improved but I was unable to get placed into the advanced history classes. I was a strait A student in all social studies classes and was a B student in all of my math classes. I was in all of the advanced math classes when I wanted to be in the advanced history classes. In my junior year, I decided to go to college and would need to take the ACT test to get into college. I bought a how to book about the ACTs. I spent six months working on vocabulary, math and English. Memory work was my forte and it didn't let me down. I took the ACT test at the local college in a very intimidating room. I did fine. I scored 25 and got a 28 in math. I was way above average.

One thing I learned in high school was how to handle money. I had quit my paper route after the summer of my 9th grade year. My parents supported me in sports and also in my academics. They would buy some of my paperback books and some of my war games. When I was sixteen I tried to get a summer job. I didn't find one and I spent that summer playing baseball with younger kids or going to the new Cedar Falls municipal pool. I was bored most of the summer because my friends had jobs and I didn't. The next summer I got a job working for Vernon Fee. He was a cement contractor who lived a few blocks from my home. He said he would pay me $1.50 an hour but when I got my first paycheck I was only getting $1.25 an hour. I didn't complain because I was afraid he would let me go. He hired about five high school kids but as the summer went on I was the only one still working for him. My father bought me a used 1959 Ford Fairlane so I could get to work. I drove this car until I got married. Most of the money I earned I put into the bank.

I didn't find the work too hard but sometimes it was strenuous. That summer we put in a lot of sidewalks and patios. From this experience, I learned how to do cement work and this would pay off later in life. A wheelbarrow full of cement was very heavy and I remember pushing one over planks to a backyard patio. Vernon Fee didn't have a pneumatic jackhammer so I had to break out concrete curbs with a sludge hammer.

A new way of making basement walls was to use wooden forms and then pour the cement into these. Then I had to hit the wooden forms with a rubber mallet to get any air bubbles out. By the time I was done I thought my arms were about to fall off. Today the forms are metal and decorative and there are easier ways to get out the bubbles. Later truckloads of sand were dumped into this formed basement. It would take hours to move the sand with a shovel and even it out. When the floor was poured I was on a rake moving the cement as the adult workers did the troweling. Knowing how to be a hard worker in the wrestling room just reinforced the idea of working hard on the job. I was asked if I would work Saturdays in the fall. I declined so that I could prepare for the wrestling season.

In my junior year David Loy had a car and I rode with him to school every day. During wrestling my parents picked me up or if I needed to lose some weight I would run the three miles home with my book bag under one arm and my coronet under the other. My senior year I had my own car but had no income. I had some money saved in the bank when Terry Meewes had an offer for me. His neighbor, Levi Siers, wanted a ride to school and not have to take the bus. In those days, it cost 15 cents per ride to or from school. If I gave Levi a ride to school he would pay me $1.35 per week. I took the offer. I now had gas money for the rest of the year. Readers should realize that gas cost less than thirty cents a gallon in those days. When wrestling ended I got a job at McDonalds making $1.00 an hour.

The job at McDonalds would influence my life. The first night on the job we had a run. A basketball tournament was taking place and when it was over hundreds of people converged on McDonalds. I was in training to be a cashier. Back then we called it to run a window. There was no inside seating and we opened up several windows to wait on customers who then took their food to their cars. The cash register did not add up amounts so we had scratch paper and a pencil to add up the amount to charge the customer. I was doing well and because of the rush I was given my own window. It didn't take long to memorize the simple menu of those days. Example: hamburger 20 cents, fries 18 cents and coke 10 cents. The two-cent tax made it 50 cents. One thing I liked was that at the end of my shift I could eat any food items of my choice. I learned to be courteous and made some new friends. I left McDonalds in the summer but would work there for three more years while I was in college.

I graduated from high school on 5 June 1967. My class rank was 105 out of 375 and I had been accepted to attend the University of Northern Iowa in Cedar Falls. This was the new name of the Iowa Normal School my grandmother attended and the Iowa State Teachers College my father attended. I had a new summer job at the Cedar Falls Municipal Utilities that paid $1.60 an hour. They hired three or four summer employees and I would be the first to ever work four summers in a row. I was assigned to the gas and water construction department. Work was much easier than working for Vernon Fee. Plus, we took a fifteen-minute "coffee break" every morning and every afternoon. This was my first experience with a union even though I was not in it. We were in a crew of three people and we took turns working. Here is an example: There is a small gas leak that needs to be repaired. A crew came the day before with a concrete saw and then our tractor man digs out the hole until he comes to the gas main. Then I dig with a shovel around the pipe and clean it off. The third man fixes the leak and then we fill in the hole. In my last year, I learned to fix the leak and so I did two of the jobs. For the coffee break we got in the truck and drove to a café. It usually took thirty minutes. This laid-back work one at a time I could get used to, but to me I saw a lot of man-hours wasted with this method. City employees really have a nice way of working to make a good salary but not if you are the taxpayer supporting it.

One summer we tore up the entire main street of downtown Cedar Falls. All of the gas mains were being replaced for new changes in the road. They gave me a dump truck and left a tractor near a large sand pile. I loaded my own truck and brought the sand to fill into the holes. Once I backed right into a hole and had to be pulled out with a tractor. I was trusted beyond any other summer part time help. Sometimes I was given my own truck and would paint fire hydrants all day. I think I painted too many each day and the job went to someone less ambitious. If an emergency required the men to work overtime a foreman took me back to the shop as I was forbidden to receive overtime pay. As the summer of 1969 was coming to a close I was asked if would work part time at the vehicle repair shop. The hours were from 5:00 p.m. to 8:00 p.m. on Monday through Thursday. I would be paid $2.00 an hour. I immediately accepted, as the hours were perfect for my college schedule. For the next two years I washed and waxed trucks at night and worked at McDonalds for $1.60 an hour during the day.

With my first summer money, I bought a brand-new Suzuki 200cc scrambler. I always rode this to school and work except in the winter or bad weather. Soon Don Johnston bought a used Yamaha 250 and Terry Meewes bought a used Honda 305. Sometimes we got together to ride over hills at a quarry and along the Cedar River. Once time we were stopped by a Park Ranger for driving in the grass in a county park. He took us to a Justice of the Peace where we were fined $25.00 each. We were careful not to ever do that again.

In the fall of 1967 I went to college to become a teacher. I was a history major so what was I going to do with that except teach. No one ever directed me to another way. I lived at home and drove to college every day. I ate breakfast and dinner at home and ate for free at McDonalds Monday through Friday. I paid for my tuition from the money I saved working every summer. The fall of 1967 cost me $66.00 for a fifteen-hour load plus books. My college routine was set. Breakfast at home, classes from 8:00 to 11:00 go to work at McDonalds until 1:30 and either take another class or go home to study until about 5:00 p.m. and have a home cooked supper. In 1969, I added the job at the utilities on Monday through Thursday. The weekends were all free time. I'll have more on that later.

I was always a serious student and never missed a class. It was my hard-earned money that paid for the classes I was taking. Every freshman has to take a humanities class. I had Prof. Alvin Sunceri for Humanities 1. The reading list for this class included ten paperbacks, which I purchased. I soon found out I could never read them all in the time allotted. Dr. Sunceri always had essay tests and gave tips about what the test questions might be. I still remember my first test question in that class. It was about the contributions to civilization from the Assyrians. I memorized all of the names of the Assyrian rulers, the dates they ruled and what each one contributed. He was floored that anyone could spell all the rulers and have their dates right plus the information he hoped to see. I got an A in that class and took every class he taught. I had a 2.67 grade point my first semester in college.

By the fall of 1969 I had a 3.0 GPA and got an A in every history class except American History where I got Bs. I had to take education classes to be a teacher and they were usually five-hour classes. I got a five-hour A twice that really helped my GPA. The books for these classes cost about $25.00 and I was not going to pay that much for a book. So, I read them at the library as one copy was on reserve. I have to admit that those classes were a waste of time. I don't remember much from those classes. In fact, those classes didn't prepare me to be a teacher at all.

My father gave me some advice in the summer of 1968 about education. If I were going to be a teacher, what would I do in the summers when school is closed? He was a guard at a factory for minimum wage and I could do better. He suggested that I take driver education classes. So, I did. I spent my sophomore and junior years taking one driver education class each semester. The first class was just on safety. The next two classes were the real things. In Driver and Traffic Safety 1 each of us had a subject that we prepared and presented to our classmates. Then we taught it to the night school class held at the college for high school students and learned how to run the simulators. In Driver and Traffic Safety 2 I was assigned a student and would teach behind the wheel instruction. We had only one car for about thirty-five of us and we had an assigned time to drive one student for twelve weeks. I was twenty years old when my sixteen-year-old female student spent an hour in the car with me every week. I can't imagine doing that today. Schools have rules today about male teachers driving with a single female student. This could be quite a liability issue.

What is really on an eighteen-year-old male's mind? Perhaps sex drugs and rock and roll. So, let's start with the least denominator: rock and roll. From about 1963 I became interested in the top 40 singles played on the radio. We only had A M radio back then and my favorite was KWWL in Waterloo. I played the radio every night when I went to bed while I read a book. When I got my car, I played the radio all the time. That was all I wanted. I never bought records or albums. I considered that a waste of money when the radio was free. I never cared for the new heavy metal but preferred love songs.

The late sixties were a time of hippies and drugs. As a serious student, I wanted to get my education and could not find the time to protest. I am not going to skip class and certainly not skip work or get fired. None of my friends ever became hippy protesters but I did know a few of them. In my junior year of college, I ran for the student senate and won. I attended the evening forums but was just loath to the hippies that controlled the congress. I was never interested in drugs or marijuana. I didn't smoke cigarettes so why should I smoke weed. I just figured drugs would mess up my routine I had made for college. However, I did get involved with beer but not hard liquor. I never bought any beer myself but some of my friends did. A group of high school friends met at Don Johnston's house every Saturday morning. His mother worked until 5:00 p.m. and he bought a case of Schlitz at the nearby store. Most of the guys were in college so we got together about 8:30 and drank beer and hung out all day. Then we went home. We did this for three years until most of us broke up or got married.

I never had another girl friend after 2nd grade. I always went to the junior high dances but they were really boring. I only went to a high school dance once. I was too shy to approach a girl. Dave Loy and I went to senior prom with each other. So, after high school I finally met some girls. Terry Meewes got a brand-new Ford Torino for graduation and we would go to Waterloo and cruise 4th Street. Right out of the movie *American Graffiti* the teenagers cruised the street and met each other. Racing was never part of this. Terry would get some beer and we now had liquid courage. My 1959 Ford was not that cool even though I had it painted metallic blue and I could drive with the headlights and parking lights on at the same time. The 1968 Dodge Charger was the first car I ever saw that could do that and was my favorite car, even though I have never owned one.

My first love was Kathy Griffith. Don Johnston had a 1960 Ford convertible when we met Kathy and Debbie Broessles on 4th Street. Kathy was nineteen and I was eighteen. She was gorgeous and had been the runner-up of the Miss Waterloo Contest. She worked in a factory and although we dated for about six weeks she realized we were different. I had invited her to the homecoming game at UNI when she broke up with me. I was heartbroken but I would get over it.

Then in the winter in 1968 I was with Terry Meewes on 4th Street when we came upon a small fender bender. I met my future wife, Bonnie Brinkman, who had just tapped the car ahead of her. Bonnie was only sixteen and was driving her parent's car up and down the strip. I got her phone number and called her the next week. We began dating, she was in high school and I was in college. She lived in a little town west of Cedar Falls, New Hartford, and in those days, that would be a long-distance phone call. It would cost fifteen cents a minute to call her. So, I called on Wednesday and we went out every Saturday, usually to the movies. A weekend routine had developed with me out with the boys on Friday and then out with Bonnie on Saturday. I still chased after a few girls but soon realized Bonnie was the one for me.

In the fall of 1968 we decided to get married but would wait until a year after she graduated from high school. We held an engagement party in her parent's basement. Terry Meewes was not there since he had joined the marines once he had gotten his draft notice. Mike Mead came and met his future wife Mary Engalls, a friend of Bonnie's. To me I never wanted to fool around with women. I was always looking for a partner to marry. Bonnie was the high school sweetheart I never had.

The Vietnam War was always in the background of my life once I graduated from high school. Of all of my childhood friends only Terry ever went into the military. I had considered joining the military my sophomore year. A Marine recruiter at the UNI campus told me of a program where I would go to boot camp after my junior year in college and after graduation I would go to Pensacola for pilot training. I would have done this if I had not met Bonnie. Marriage and career were the goals that drove me in my decision-making and I had a routine of work, school and dating that would lead me to achieve my goals. So, in late 1969 I turned in my student deferment draft card for a 1A card. The draft lottery numbers had already been drawn and I had number 250. The draft had never gone beyond number 180 so I felt safe. I was right. I did not get drafted.

In 1969, I was twenty years old and had goals for my life. I continued to go to church every Sunday and never skipped a day of school. I had been sick in 7th grade for a week but after that I had perfect attendance through high school and would never miss a class in college. I was not very aware of the world around me and lived in a bubble. Once I went to college I stopped watching television because I had no time for it. Martin Luther King, the civil rights movement and even the hippies didn't mean much to me. I was on a path to marriage and a career and drugs and politics would just get in the way. I was definitely a law and order person and a tribute to my parents. I made enough money from my summer job to pay for school and made enough money from my McDonalds job to pay for gas and a few nights out. I even put money in the bank. The choices I made in this part of my life set the tone for the rest of my life. I chose to not do drugs or to smoke anything. I had a few peer pressure moments that I lost but certainly learned from. My awareness of the rest of the world would soon be upon me.

CHAPTER 5

The 1970's

Building a Family and Career

On 4 June 1970 Bruce Robert Kindig married Bonnie Jean Brinkman at St John Lutheran Church in Cedar Falls, Iowa. Don Johnston was my best man. Bonnie had her sister as her Matron of Honor. We went on a honeymoon to Jamaica. This was the first time I had ever flown in an airplane. I had saved the $1100.00 to do this. When we returned home I went back to work at the Cedar Falls Utilities for the summer and Bonnie worked as a waitress at Marc's Big Boy. We rented an apartment at 709 Main St. in Cedar Falls for $85.00 a month and now we were responsible for all of the bills.

As I started my senior year of college we established a new routine. Bonnie would work to pay the rent and groceries and I would continue to work nights at the Utilities washing trucks. I gave up the McDonalds job because I was going to be student teaching in November. As a married couple, we didn't see our friends very often. Don Johnston got married in November and I didn't even know he had been dating. I was his best man and he had dropped out of college the year before. He worked as the manager of a warehouse and except for our ten-year class reunion I never saw him again. Mike Mead also married Mary Engalls and the last time I saw him was in 1972. Terry Meewes got out of the Marines in late 1970. One night he woke me up at 2:00 a.m. He had bought an El Camino and drove it to Kansas City to buy Coors beer. That was the closest place to us that Coors distributed back then. We spent some time carrying forty cases of Coors upstairs to my apartment. I would see Terry several more times in my life but it was apparent that childhood friends were disappearing in my life. David Loy sent me Christmas cards for many years. I did see him at my father's funeral in 2012 and he passed away in 2018.

Student teaching is not a good financial situation. Student teachers were not allowed to work and had to pay the tuition cost of the program. I worked washing trucks at the Cedar Falls Utilities at night as I had for the past two years and I did not tell anyone. Miss Marie Shellard was my mentor at West High School in Waterloo, Iowa. She was in her sixties and really didn't help me very much. She had a tendency to correct my mistakes in front of the class; which didn't make me feel very good. Another teacher, Bill Blake, was much more helpful but West High School was very much like the school I graduated from. The socio-economic background of the students was very middle class and I never had any disciplinary incidents. There were no lesson plans but rather teacher lecture notes. The teacher-student relationship was great and if all students were like the ones I had at West High School, teaching would be great. One thing I learned was to be friendly, fair but firm. This would become my calling card as a teacher. I finished student teaching in late January 1971 and still had one semester of college to finish.

My last semester at UNI was very routine; I washed trucks at night and went to school during the day. I carried fifteen hours of studies including a two-hour course called Directing a Safety Program. The director of the Safety Education curriculum was Ivan Eland. Dr. Eland was well known in the safety field and had connections all over the state of Iowa. He let me know about a job opportunity to teach driver education in the summer of 1971 in Marion, Iowa. I applied for the job and was accepted to start in June. I informed the Cedar Falls Utilities that I would not be back to work part time summers for them. I gave up a $2.00 per hour job for a $6.00 per hour job. I would now have more responsibilities to teach driving to thirty-four teenagers. I should point out to readers, that throughout my driver education career the teacher pay was usually three times the minimum wage.

I spent time in my last semester applying for teaching jobs. I attended career fairs and went to meetings with school recruiters. Everything was falling into place except that I had no offers to be a full-time teacher. I graduated from UNI in late May, 1971 with a B.A. degree in history with a teaching credential. I had a minor in Safety Education and was certified to teach government as well. I finished four years of college with a 3.1 GPA and never failed a class. My memory work had paid off. I still did not have a job offer for the fall and I had sent out seventy applications. The best paying jobs were in Alaska and Chicago. They would pay a starting teacher $10,000 per year. I had two weeks between graduation and the start of my summer driver ed. job to work on my applications. One morning I had decided to make some phone calls and I would concentrate on finding a job in Iowa. I had called a half a dozen schools with no results when my phone rang. It was a call from the Davenport Community School District and they wanted me to come for an interview. I said yes and I went the next day.

I had never been to Davenport when I came for an interview. I met with the curriculum director Daryl Leitz and then he took me to Frank L. Smart Junior High School where I met with the principal, George Latta. Mr. Latta was about 60-years old and gave me a tour of the school, which was still in session. I completed the interview and was offered a job on the spot. I had no other prospective interviews and this offer was now or never. I accepted the job to teach 7th Grade social studies for $7300.00 per year. The school year would start in late August so I had some time to plan for my move to Davenport.

Later that week I drove to Marion, Iowa to meet my driver ed. students and their parents. I had already prepared a driving schedule and I would work 40 hours per week. The schedule was 8:00 a.m. to 5:00 p.m. Monday through Friday with one hour off for lunch. I found a mobile home park in Marion where I could park my parent's travel trailer for $25.00 per month. Bonnie quit her job at Marc's Big Boy and we both moved to Marion to live in a small trailer for six weeks. I had to prepare my classroom lessons in the evening and drove students all day. I was 22 years old and my students were 15 or 16. I drove students on two lane highways at 70 mph, which was the speed limit in those days. I also drove into Cedar Rapids and taught the students how to use a standard stick shift transmission. We usually went to Bonnie's parents' home on the weekends. I finished the course without incident and saved most of the money I earned from the job. I would not see another paycheck until 15 September.

When driver education ended Bonnie and I went with her parents to Wyoming for a little vacation. Except for my honeymoon I had not taken a vacation for the past six years. The ranch of Delbert Jones was a regular place for my father-in-law to go hunting in the fall. Jones was a sheep rancher and lived sixty miles from the nearest town. I returned there seven or eight years later to find that Jones was now in the oil business. Oil had been discovered on his land and he now read meters for the company. When we returned to Iowa we went to Davenport to look for an apartment. I had a hard time finding Smart Junior High that I had seen a couple months ago. Once I found it we went looking for an apartment close enough that I could walk to school. Smart is located in a blue-collar area that I was not used to. The socio-economics of my students was not going to be what I expected. We finally settled on a nice apartment on Jebens Ave. which was in a more middle-class neighborhood and too far for me to walk to work. The rent was $185.00 per month and I had to pay for two months in advance. We left our apartment in Cedar Falls, hired a moving truck, and moved to Davenport. My career was about to begin.

Before I begin the story of my career and family, I feel that this would be a good place to discuss the economics of the 1970's. The Vietnam War would end in my second year of teaching. Inflation of the 60's would continue into the 70's. Minimum wage would rise from $2.00 in 1970 to $2.90 in 1979. The oil crisis in 1973 and again in 1979 would affect the cost of gasoline driving up the price from 30 cents per gallon to $1.00 per gallon. Usually my wages stayed ahead of inflation and I slowly accumulated wealth in the form of property not in cash.

In 1971, I bought my first car. It was a new 1971 Pontiac LeMans two-door coupe with a vinyl roof. I paid $3700 for the car and took out my first loan. I had always wanted a Dodge Charger but a new Charger was over $4000 and the dealer would not go lower. I had given my old 1959 Ford to my father when I got married and he drove it for several years until he junked it. I sold my motorcycle to a 16-year-old just before I graduated from college. I heard he was in a car-motorcycle accident a few months later. I had been driving my wife's 1969 Mustang since we were married. So, this Pontiac was my first "new" car. I probably should have waited on this purchase as it put a strain on my finances. The $7300 yearly salary of a beginning teacher turned out to be $444.00 per month net pay. Here are some early figures for life in 1971: rent-$185, car payment- $70, heating and cooling- $20, telephone $15 (plus long-distance calls), insurance $50, gasoline $20. That left us about $100 for food and clothing. The problem with a teacher's paycheck is that there are only twelve of them in a year. My first check would be on 1 October but since I would have been working for six weeks without any pay I received half of it on 15 September. By 1 November I had been working for ten weeks on $444.00. Our financial situation was strained. The $444.00 I got on 1 November only had $50.00 for us to spend on groceries.

In September 1971 Bonnie looked for work. She got a job as a waitress at a nice restaurant in downtown Davenport called the Italian Village. She made $1.25 per hour plus tips. She also sold Avon for a while as well as Beeline Fashions. This was a home party clothing sales job. Our school had an evening program for disadvantaged kids where we opened up the gymnasium for exercise and games. I took a $3.00 per hour job supervising the gym with three other teachers. We could not continue this lifestyle so we decided to move. In February 1972, we moved to a house on W. 70th Street even further from my work. The rent was $140.00 and we caught up with our bills. I would get pay raises every year that I was a teacher and the pay increase would be even larger if I had an advanced degree. I was turned down by the Davenport Community School District to teach summer driver education so I decided to go back to UNI and work on a Master's Degree.

Each summer of 1972-73-74 Bonnie and I would live with my parents in Cedar Falls while I attended summer school. I rode my old bicycle to graduate school every day. I took classes in the morning and studied and wrote papers in the afternoon for eight weeks. I took a class from my old mentor Alvin Sunceri that first summer. It was entitled "War and Society in the Modern World." I excelled in my memory work as usual but the term paper I wrote was over 100 pages. I still can't believe I had the time to complete that plus all of my other class work. I took nine semester hours that summer and was definitely overworked. I had taken six hours of an education class in the spring so I now had a BA+15 that was a double move on the salary schedule.

In my second year of teaching I made $8500 and felt pretty good about our finances. That year I also took a job coaching the 7th and 8th grade combined wrestling team at Smart. I had helped the coach the year before but he wanted to get out of coaching. My old desire to wrestle told me to ask for the position. Without any coaching experience, I got the job. The season was only six weeks long and I got paid $300.00. I continued going to summer school at UNI and graduated with a M.A. degree in history in 1974. This degree would guarantee me at least $1000.00 a year for the rest of my career. By 1975 my teaching career was making over $10,000 a year and would continue to improve ahead of inflation.

I should mention how I achieved a master's degree in history. I had to select three areas of history to focus on. I chose ancient history, modern European history, and modern U.S. history. Before graduation I would have to take a three-hour written exam in each area and take a one-hour oral exam at UNI with a panel of professors. It was the biggest challenge for my memory work. I met several people in this program that quit before they took exams because of the rigor. I had never taken a course in ancient history so I enrolled in a Roman History class. For ancient Greece and the Middle Ages, I bought some textbooks and taught myself these subjects. I prepared note cards and memorized the facts as well as the opinions of historians. Just as I had studied for the ACT test in high school I now spent six months studying for my written exams. I would spend one hour per day studying the note cards I prepared. The written exam would be on a Saturday morning, Saturday afternoon and a Sunday morning. The Social Studies Department Head, Jerry Conyers, agreed to be my proctor. The Thursday before the exam I called in sick and spent the entire day studying my note cards. I was prepared for some fifty topics and I knew every note card by heart. For six hours on Saturday and three hours on Sunday I wrote on nine subjects selected by the UNI professors without any notes. I was prepared for every one of those questions and passed with flying colors. Later I went to Cedar Falls for the orals but that was easy compared to the written test. They were all pleased with my responses and awarded me the degree. My thesis was about forty pages and was entitled "Peace Proposals of World War I." I could now teach at the college level should I ever want to.

As my income increased I invested in property. I examined some new houses in 1971 hoping I would qualify for a government program called 235-I. This program would grant a lower interest rate and make the house more affordable for low-income people. I didn't qualify because I made $300.00 a year above the poverty level. I did buy a house at 5904 Hillandale Road in 1973 for $20,000. It was only two years old and had an eight percent thirty-year mortgage with a payment of $154.00 per month. It was only nine dollars more than I was paying for rent. It was a story and a half with an unfinished upstairs and basement. There also was no garage. Everyone on our block were young couples with children. I quickly made friends and my next-door neighbor Dennis Anderson had a wood shop next to his house. This would come in handy over the years.

I intended to build two bedrooms in the upstairs of our new house. Whenever I saw 2 X 4s on sale I would buy what I could. I would buy a few sheets of plywood now and then and would start laying down the floor. However, the first real project I tackled was to build a garage. I persuaded Dennis Anderson to help me build it. The two of us would do it in three weeks. In August 1975, I took out a building loan and bought a one and a half car unattached garage from Payless Cashway. They delivered all of the materials in one big pile in my back yard. Meanwhile, I used my cement skills I had learned in my first job and Dennis and I poured a floating slab and extended my driveway. The whole thing was finished before the start of the school year and it was well constructed. Two years later I reciprocated with Dennis when he added a two-car attached garage to his house. I did the cement work and helped build with the construction.

I finished the first bedroom upstairs in 1978 and the other one in 1979. I did all of the work myself, except the electrical that Dennis Anderson did for me. When my parents had built the upstairs bedroom when I was a child, my grandfather Louis Kindig had made some built in drawers in the walls and had made built in desks. My new bedrooms now had those very same features. I am sure my junior high shop teachers would have been proud of me. The smaller room became my study and the larger room became a bedroom for my two oldest children. I never finished the basement but I did put in a shower because there was no shower on the main floor. In 1981, I added central air conditioning.

I had set goals to finish college and get married. In the 1970's I set up some different goals for my life. The first goal I have already mentioned, to complete a M.A. degree in history. I also set a goal to read twenty-five books a year. During my college days, I had no time to read what I wanted as the reading list of the professors was actually too much. I joined a couple of book of the month clubs and slowly began my library. Today I have over 1000 books that I have accumulated. My third goal was to write a book before the decade was out. I actually finished the book in 1979. It was entitled "The French and Indian War, The First World War." I sent several copies to publishers, but it was never published.

My teaching career had a rough start. College had not prepared me for what was ahead. I knew my subject very well but the application of the teaching process was difficult. To be friendly, I always greeted my students at the door of the classroom and tried to greet them by name. Since I had 150 students this was quite the challenge. I knew most of them in three weeks. To be fair I ran a double grade book of points and grades. This was very cumbersome and time consuming and I used only the point method after my first year. I remained firm in my decisions and policies and from that I soon would see a student loyalty to my sincerity. They saw that I cared about them and everything that I did was for their benefit.

In my first year, I taught 7th grade world geography and history. Another new teacher, John Pagan, had recently graduated from Marycrest College but was hired after me. I had my own classroom but he had to travel between rooms and taught 7th and 8th grade curriculums. I didn't realize it at the time but I had seniority over him and therefore I had some privileges. There will be more on this topic later. The 7th grade curriculum was a mild world history class with emphasis on geography. The lessons in the curriculum guide were not well thought out and I never used them. Every lesson in my first year I had to make from scratch. I got no help from any of the other teachers. The textbook was over five years old and somewhat beat up. There were only thirty copies of the text so all reading had to be done in class. I had no supplies because everything would have been ordered the year before. My department head, Jerry Conyers gave me ten reams of paper. This was not nearly enough for 150 students for a year. Jerry also gave me a file drawer in the bottom of his file cabinet. I didn't have a file cabinet or any place to keep any papers.

I was 22 years old and my students were 12 or 13; just a ten-year difference. They were baby boomers like myself and the school was crowded to the maximum. This increase in students every year would continue for about three more years until the number of students began to decline, partly because a new junior high building was under construction. They also had different backgrounds than I did. They came from blue-collar homes and many were poor. Up until this point I would carry money in my wallet or pocket. So many of them asked to "borrow" money for lunch that I soon didn't have any myself. I seldom carried money to school again. I also had my first encounter with minorities. I only had two black students that first year. Smart Junior High had a small Hispanic population and I got to know all of these students very well. My philosophy of friendly, fair and firm works on everyone and I enjoyed all of my students.

With all of the deficits to my new job I plunged ahead. I only had two problems my first year. First, a boy named Gary. He was quite the problem and I could not get him to behave. I decided to make a home visit and once Gary saw me in his house taking an interest in him he made a change. He was as good as could be and began doing his lessons and was quite successful. The second student was a boy named David. He never caused any problems like Gary but just sat in his seat and did absolutely nothing. I had never seen anyone do nothing in school on purpose. I never connected with him and he was the only student that failed my class in my first year.

Some of my lessons didn't work well. I was using many of the techniques I used as a student teacher and they just didn't work. The students were great. Many of them came and talked to me and I think they liked me as I had some popularity. By the second semester of my first year I began to connect my lessons with the students. Things fell into place and I was sure that I could succeed as a teacher. After talking to the principal, George Latta, he was able to get me a file cabinet, more paper and school supplies that I needed. I had already spent my own money to purchase colored pencils for the students to use on their map assignments. At the end of my first year I was asked if I wanted to transfer to a new junior high building, Wallace Wood Junior High that was opening because of the increased enrollment. I said no, I wanted to teach 7th grade at Smart again and this time do it right.

I continued to teach 7th grade for the next two years. I really enjoyed the students and my lessons worked well. However, this was not what I wanted to teach. I wanted to teach history and that is where all of my background was. I was also completing my master's degree in history. I had asked for a transfer to West High School in Davenport but it never went anywhere. I even had an interview with the principal as I had seen several math teachers transfer from Smart to West. This is when I saw the failure of my teacher's union. First, I did not have enough seniority with only three years' experience. Second, I would never get a transfer under this system because I was doing too well at being a junior high teacher. The people that got transferred were one's that the principal wanted to get rid of because they were not very good at the junior high level. I know that unions negotiate for salaries but in Iowa the salaries are based on the amount of taxes collected. You can't get paid more than they have. One year I only got a $50.00 raise. That was so disheartening. At least I still got my step increase.

At the end of the 1973-74 school year we experienced the first effect of a decline in enrollment. Since the opening of Wood Junior High pressure was taken off of the other schools. Smart would have to cut one social studies position. I had six days seniority over John Pagan and he was transferred to Wood.

The new principal at Smart was Jim Dexter. He was very personable and I liked him very much. He knew I wanted to teach history so he moved me to teach 8th grade American Studies. This was a U.S. History from 1492 to 1820 class with a mini course in African-American studies and a mini course in economics. Now I finally was going to teach what I wanted; and there was a textbook for every student. The curriculum was well worked out with some interesting lessons. I will teach this for the next thirteen years. Jim Dexter also put me in charge of the detention hall after school. He gave me the authority to call parents and threaten suspension if they didn't show up. I never had a problem with these students because of my reputation. I wasn't mean; I was fair and firm. I only had to make a few phone calls.

I was not satisfied teaching at Smart Junior High. Some things had changed in the classroom. Students had become unruly. I now had more students who didn't want to learn. I never really had problems with these students but they no longer wanted to connect to education. One student named Steve came to school once every ten days. When I asked him about his attendance he told me he came to school just often enough to keep his mother out of jail. Others didn't seem to have the reading skills to cope. More and more students were coming to 8th grade with only 3rd grade reading levels and they did not want to do remedial work. So, in 1975 I went looking for another school district. I went to Dubuque, Iowa to a parochial school called Wahlert High School. Dubuque is a nice town and Wahlert belonged to the Catholic diocese. I was offered a job to teach their 9th grade geography class. There were three reasons why I turned them down. First, the Geography classroom was long and narrow and I would have up to sixty students in each class. Davenport had a maximum of thirty per class. Second, I asked about the pension program and was told that it was two percent of your pay and that no one had ever retired. Finally, the pay was much lower than I was making in Davenport. I also went to Boone, Iowa for a job in the high school. The old high school building was as dilapidated as Smart, if not worse. The facilities were under par and I didn't like what I saw. Besides, they wanted me to coach their 9th grade wrestling team at the local YMCA a block away. I did not like that situation. On top of that the pay was much lower than Davenport. I decided to stay in Davenport and finish my career there.

On the very last day of the 1976-77 school year, Ted Curtis, the Social Studies Coordinator for the district came into my classroom. My students were doing some fun activities and I was making balloon animals. He came to tell me that I was being transferred to Williams Junior High for next year and needed to see the principal there at the end of the day. He never did say anything to me about the balloons. I met Bob Van Dyke that afternoon and I would be teaching 8th grade American Studies at Williams. At the end of the 1977-78 school year my replacement at Smart was cut and she lost her job because she had no seniority over anyone.

I would teach 8th grade American Studies for the next ten years at Williams Junior High. In 1977, I was the lowest in seniority so I had to be the traveling teacher. Williams had very few minorities and was more middle class than Smart and the students were all well behaved. I couldn't believe the difference. One day I encountered a student smoking in the rest room. If this happened at Smart I would have to escort the student to the office, but in this case the student went straight to the office to turn himself in with me tagging behind him. Everything ran smoothly and I enjoyed teaching at Williams much more than I did at Smart. I never sent any student to the principal's office for disciplinary reasons. I always handled my own situations.

In the 1970s my career added two more paths. I began a twenty-six-year career as a wrestling coach and I would find a driver education job in the summer that would last for thirty-one years.

With my interest in wrestling I had asked George Latta at Smart if I could be a wrestling coach. Young teachers often became coaches to supplement their income and I was no exception. In 1972, I became the 7th and 8th grade combined wrestling coach. We had a new practice area in the balcony of the gym. I had about 30 wrestlers and everyone got to wrestle as we always arranged extra matches. I used what I knew in my coaching, that is I trained the athletes as I had learned from Coach Dotson. There were no laundry facilities at the school and I couldn't trust the wrestlers to bring back a clean uniform for the next meet. Therefore, I carried the clothes home and laundered them myself. Smart was known for their tough athletes and we did pretty good that first year. One thing I noticed, however, was the poor performance of the referees. So, I decided to become a wrestling referee.

The next year I began taking coaching classes and I took the test to become a referee. Within a year I was a certified coach and started refereeing. The wrestling schedule was lengthened and was no longer a short exercise. In 1975, I became the 9th grade coach and Mike Wood, a science teacher, took over the 7th and 8th grade team. We now had new mats like everyone recognizes today. When I started we had horsehair mats with a plastic cover. The 9th grade practiced in the cafeteria and we had to roll the mats out for each practice and roll them back up when we were done. Davenport did not allow 9th graders to practice or compete at the high school level. Because of that a city tournament was the high point of a junior high wrestler. I didn't realize the affect I had upon my athletes until Todd Marsden was injured during the city tournament. I had to decide if he should default the match when he said to me "I can wrestle, I don't want to let you down." He was wrestling for me and not for himself. For his safety, I had him default the match. I found this kind of loyalty throughout my coaching career.

When I transferred to Williams Junior High in 1977 I thought I would give up my coaching. I was now refereeing high school meets and gaining a good reputation for fairness. Roger Keester, the P.E. teacher at Williams was the 9th grade wrestling coach and approached me about taking over the team. I accepted. Williams had the best wrestling room of all the junior highs in Davenport. A new school in 1956 it had a designated wrestling room with a separate locker room. I would never have facilities better than this. The room even had a heater so the wrestlers could sweat off some weight. Williams did not have a very strong wrestling program and usually finished last in the city tournament. There were only about fifteen wrestlers on the team and we actually did very well that first season. The next two years I increased the size of the team by doing some recruiting in my classroom and in the study halls. What I couldn't do as a wrestler I was able to do as a coach. I inspired the athletes to do their best and I always had some champions, something that Williams had not seen for a while. One time I had a parent ask me why his son wasn't in the starting lineup. I told him we had wrestle offs every Friday and the winners would be the starters. I invited him to come and watch the wrestle offs. He never did show up. I never picked the team but allowed everyone the opportunity to earn a starting spot. Everyone wrestled off on Friday. I would never allow anyone to be treated as I had been in my senior year of high school.

For the summer of 1975 I was looking for a driver education job. I tried to get hired in my own school district but I didn't have the right connections. So, I sent out applications to various districts around Davenport. The town of DeWitt is located about twenty miles north of Davenport and this is where I found a job. Neil Padgett was the driver education teacher at the school and always hired someone to help him in the summer. I interviewed with the principal, Howard Ehlers, and was hired for what would become thirty-one summers. Neil became a very good friend of mine until his death in 2001. The local dealer provided two new Buicks for us to use.

My first summer at DeWitt I had forty-five students that I had to drive with. I could not get all of the students done in the six weeks we had scheduled and had to work another week. I was making $7.00 per hour and DeWitt allowed students to miss drives although they still had to be made up. I didn't mind since this increased my pay but the hours were long and I was usually very tired by the end of the day. The next year we added a third instructor. Pat Spurgeon was a gym teacher at Ekstrand Elementary School in Dewitt and Pat and I would work together for many years.

In 1977 through 1979 Neil decided to sell insurance instead of doing driver education. I now became the instructor in charge. We hired Bruce Kimbrell from Corning, Iowa as our third instructor. This was good experience for me in running a driver education program. It also meant that I had to do some work at home preparing as well as typing up all of the completion slips. Wages had gone up to $9.00 per hour. I now had a good supplement to my income and it was steady. I also bought a 1968 VW bug for $500.00 so Bonnie would have a car while I was in DeWitt. I drove the bug.

While I was working on my career I was also working on my family. Daniel Bruce Kindig was born on 29 June 1973 in Davenport. I was in Cedar Falls at the time taking classes. Bonnie remained in Davenport and her mother was staying with her. When I got the call that she was going to the hospital I delayed leaving for a couple hours. I had studied for a Roman History exam so I went to take the exam and then left for Davenport. My father went with me and we went to the hospital. Daniel was a cute red head. I did get an A on the Roman History test. We had moved into our home on Hillandale the previous April and we had the baby bedroom ready.

Rebecca Ann Kindig was born on 21 April 1976 in Davenport. She also had red hair and with two children I needed to make some changes. We needed a bigger car, so I traded my LeMans for a new 1976 Ford station wagon. Now we had plenty of room for traveling. I also doubled my efforts to finish the rooms upstairs. Joshua Robert Kindig was born on 14 December 1979 in Davenport.

The family was complete and all of the goals I set for myself had been accomplished. I still continued my war-gaming hobby but I had given up on the play by mail situation. Bob Malake, a teacher at Smart, had invited me to play poker with a bunch of fellows one evening. At his house, I noticed he had a number of Avalon Hill games. The two of us became instant game buddies and we played as often as we could.

Bonnie and I joined Prince of Peace Lutheran Church in 1972 and had all of our children baptized there. Once the kids starting going to Sunday School so did we. I read in the church bulletin about a church softball league. With my baseball background, I decided to get some activity in my life. There was one catch to the church softball league. If I wanted to play I would have to be the coach. I accepted and went to the house of the previous coach to get the equipment. I still remember thinking about his house when I arrived. A $50,000 two-story house, it would be perfect for my family if only I could afford it. I was now a player coach of a softball team. I now had driver education during the day and softball on several evenings.

I had a full life and a comfortable life. I had a family and a full-time teaching job and I supplemented my income with some coaching as well as a summer job. I made enough money to put some into bonds for my children's education. When opportunities came I evaluated the situation and made a life choice. I had learned enough skills to do carpentry as well as cement work and these improved the value of my home. There were no major illnesses or injuries and my insurance paid all of the maternity costs. I had never missed a day of work except the day I took to study for my exams. It wasn't all work as I still looked forward to a little vacation. Except for long weekends I only had early August for travel. We didn't travel much at first. We went to Minnesota fishing twice, revisited Delbert Jones in Wyoming with a stop in the Black Hills and in 1976 we went to Six Flags near St. Louis. We took a trip to western Pennsylvania in 1979 and we camped in a tent.

CHAPTER 6

The 1980's

The Reagan Dividend

One evening in April of 1980 I got a phone call from Earl Monholland. Earl worked for the city of Davenport as a grounds caretaker. I had met him the previous fall at the Village of East Davenport when I visited the Civil War Muster at Lindsey Park. Earl had a seven-barrel volley-gun, a somewhat rare Civil War gun. I had forgotten all about meeting him but he had my number and wanted to know if I would like to do some Civil War reenacting. I was very intrigued and said yes. He was going to hold a meeting at his home with some people about forming a reenacting unit. After I hung up I called my friend Boyd Ayres and together we went to the meeting.

I met Boyd when I was in college. We met at a Bar-B-Q at Professor Sunceri's home. When I moved to Davenport I discovered that Boyd had gotten a teaching job at Williams Junior High. When I transferred to Williams my first two class periods were right across the hall from Boyd's class. In 1979 Boyd and I had tried to start a reenactment group of Continental Marines. I already owned a Brown Bess musket and a friend of Boyd's took us out and we shot the Brown Bess at targets. We then decided it would be fun to relive history in full uniforms. We advertised a meeting at the Putnam Museum in Davenport, passed out flyers to about a dozen people who came and explained what we were going to do. Nobody joined. We had done it all wrong expecting people to pay hundreds of dollars to set this up.

So, we met Earl and about six other people and Earl explained how we would make our own uniforms and get all of our gear ready. We would meet several more times with the fourth of July weekend to be our first reenactment. The name of our group would be the 13th Tennessee Regiment and we would be Confederate. Earl said we would go as rebels as it was less expensive and we didn't have to match up our clothing with each other. Besides, there were no other Confederate units in the area but there were several Union ones. Earl said we would be artillery so we made our own red kepis and put red trim on our clothing. A year later we realized this was all wrong but Earl was just going by some pictures he had seen.

I bought wool at the fabric store and Bonnie sewed up my uniform. At the same time, she made herself a camp dress as well as a ball gown complete with a hoop skirt. I wore wellington boots and a red tee shirt as well. Not real authentic, but it would pass. I wanted a cap and ball revolver but couldn't come up with the $75.00 to buy it. I figured a way to raise the money. I went to my parent's home and collected up all of my old toys when I was a kid and brought them home. It was my baseball cards that bought that revolver. In fact, over the next couple years I sold all of the baseball cards making almost $2000.00.

The first reenactment was in Rockford, Illinois and I had a blast. It was a four-day weekend and we had a battle every day. Earl showed up with three Coe horn mortars that he had made. They were made of steel and Boyd and I were given one of them. There was live cannon firing and I entered the cap and ball revolver shoot. I took first place and have the trophy prominently displayed at home. I fell in love with this hobby and went to thirteen more reenactments that first year.

The 1980's were a good time to live in the United States. Inflation finally came under control and uncertain things like gasoline shortages ended. Davenport had lost a major industry in 1979. Caterpillar closed its doors and sold their property. However, the economy stabilized and my family continued to live a good life. The whole family participated in and enjoyed camping with friends at the reenactments. Over time I improved my costume.

The economy of the 1980s was much better than before. My teacher pay would double to nearly $40,000 a year. The driver education job ended the decade around $14.00 an hour and I had a secure position. Gasoline prices dropped below the one-dollar mark and that made travel expenses more manageable. Bonnie took a part time job working at a kitchen supply store to make some extra money for our new hobby. In 1983, we sold our house on Hillandale for $50,000. I paid off $5,000 in credit card debt and paid off the mortgage. We bought a new house on Forest Rd. for $76.000. I put nearly $30,000 down on the new house and we were debt free. Interesting note that this house was only one block from the house where I picked up the softball equipment. I had our dream house, a four-bedroom two-story with a family room and a fireplace. Within a year I would finish off the basement. I had a thirty-year mortgage at 11

¾ percent interest. The $650.00 a month payments were doable but I had to refinance the house five years later and got an eight percent mortgage.

I made a mistake in 1986 when I purchased a new 1985 Chevy conversion van. It was priced at $20,000 and fit all of my family needs. Five of us could travel and everyone had plenty of room. I could also carry a lot of my reenactment gear. The mistake was that I just went over budget. I had no debt before 1986 and had even taken a three-week vacation to Canada with the family in 1984. Now I would continue to carry a debt, mostly on credit cards.

In 1987, I heard about a couple of part time job opportunities. The first one was a Driver Improvement Program or DIPs. This was part of the driver licensing in Iowa where people with three moving violations could take a class to go on probation instead of losing their license. It paid $18.00 an hour and met on a Saturday for eight hours. I did a few of every year and I had to listen to the gripes and complaints people had against traffic law enforcement. By the time they left, most of them thanked me for changing their mind about traffic laws. I had eight hours to convince them that how they drove was their choice. Bad choices have consequences and they were my examples. The other job was called the homework hotline. I was paid $13.00 an hour to help students with their social studies homework over the phone. I worked with five other people at a phone bank at the local area education agency. Both of these jobs helped with the bills but I also found that they were very rewarding to me as I was able to help people.

In 1980, I got my own classroom at Williams Junior High. It was a modular classroom behind the gym. There were three of these trailers and I had a few classes in them before as the traveling teacher. The nice thing was that I controlled my own heating and air-conditioning. That's right, I now had air-conditioning. The drawback was that the trailers were far from other classes and I didn't see another adult all-day except when I went into the building. The area where my classroom was a favorite place for students to sneak out for a cigarette. That soon came to an end. I was also given all of the advanced classes of American Studies, which meant all of the better students. My friend Boyd Ayres had these classes but they were taken from him after it was determined that he did not challenge them with advanced materials as he was supposed to.

I spent five years in the trailer and it was possibly the best five years of my teaching career. I developed and improved the curriculum and instituted many of the teaching techniques that I became known for. I truly enjoyed the students in the trailer and even had some 9th grade students I got out of study hall to work on some projects for me. They say that all good things must come to an end, so in 1985 I moved back into the building as the modular units were being removed. I took over my friend Boyd Ayres classroom.

In the winter of 1985 Boyd Ayres disappeared. He did not show up for work and no one knew where he was. Even his daughter, who was a student at Williams, did not know where he was. His car had been found a short distance from the Quad-Cities Airport but there were no clues. A day later another teacher gave a letter to the principal at Williams. Boyd had given it to him to give to the principal if he did not hear from him. The letter was Boyd's resignation. But, where was he? In the teaching profession pay raises are based on seniority and education level. Boyd had a B.A. degree with twelve steps whereas I had a M.A. degree with sixteen steps and two lateral steps. Boyd was no longer getting pay raises and had chosen to work in the army reserve instead of working toward a M.A. degree. He was now too old to stay in the reserves and had cashed in his insurance policies. He was broke and teaching was not making it for him. I'm sure there were some marital issues as well. Over time he was discovered in San Francisco. He had met a nurse during summer camp and flew out to meet her. His wife divorced him and he lived with the nurse in South Carolina and might have married her. Boyd started a new career as a paralegal assistant. He died in 2018 at the age of seventy-six.

The year 1985 was also the opening of a new high school in Davenport. North High School would take off the pressure of overcrowding at the two high schools in Davenport. With this new school also brought new boundaries for the junior high schools. The new mix of students at Williams now began to resemble some of the features I saw developing when I left Smart. There was more student complacency and the desire to not learn anything. The baby boomers had been gone from my classrooms for several years, but this idea of laziness and disrespect for adult authority was becoming more prevalent. I still taught with my usual vigor and variety of lessons but some students were not moved.

I took on a different class in 1986. I became an ESL teacher. I had no training as an English as a second language teacher but our school had an influx of students from Vietnam and Cambodia. The principal, Jim Spencer, asked me to take over the social studies for these students. I was obviously a top choice for the principal and I can't see anyone else doing this from within our building. It was only one class each day and I had to develop the program. The students had already picked an English name and they would help me when language was an issue. I developed a curriculum from a 6th grade geography book. These students wanted nothing less than an A and were well behaved. This was a nice island of calm and friendly competition at Williams.

At the end of the 1987 school year I went to a teacher-bidding meeting. I had never been to one before but was told that this could go on well into the night. This was a district/union meeting to allow people to change jobs based only on seniority. I had sixteen years' experience and was looking for a change. A social studies position came up at North High School. I put in my bid and won. There were no other bids but another teacher told me he was going to bid except when he saw me put in my bid he decided he couldn't beat me. Actually, he had more experience than me but I think my reputation helped me. I was done by 7:30 p.m. and went home. Jim Spencer was not pleased that I had bid out, as I was one of his top teachers. He now had to prepare a bid for my old position.

When I got to North High School I found out that I was the lowest in seniority in the Social Studies Department. I did not have to be a traveling teacher but I was not able to choose any of my classes. I would teach three sections of geography, two sections of Applied Economics and be the teacher in charge of the student government. Not exactly the classes I expected but I had finally arrived at the high school level where I had always wanted to be.

North High School was very diverse. When it opened anyone could apply to go to this school. The school was about twenty-five percent black and fifteen percent Hispanic. Race, color, sex, religion or creed had never been a concern of mine. The first thing I discovered was how friendly all of the students were. I couldn't believe how polite everyone was. There is a big difference between junior high and senior high student behavior. Wow. My junior high experience was beneficial but now I had to prepare for three new assignments. By the time I retired I would teach twelve different subjects at North High School. The next year I was also teaching the Economics class.

Student government was a lot of work. It only met three times a week but was responsible for many activities. This required me to be present at numerous evening events and sometimes on Saturday. I created committees and they elected the leaders who were in charge of the activity. We used parliamentary procedures one day a week for a formal meeting so everyone was informed. I tried to get out of teaching this class after the first year. The principal, Paul Johnson, said he would try. He didn't try and I went on to teach this class for eleven years. This was the first time, but not the last time, a principal lied to me.

In 1989 there was a drop of enrollment at North High School. The principal wanted to keep me on the staff, so he did some shifting of my schedule. I would still have the Applied Economics class and the student government but I would now become the SWS teacher for social studies. I found this out on the first day of school. Paul Johnson had told me in May that my assignment would not change. Another lie, he knew things were changing and I had spent the summer working on the economics curriculum. School within a school is a philosophy that to prevent dropouts in high school we need to give students a second chance. I had a class of eight to ten students that I taught and I also went with them to science class particularly to help with lab work. I also had a period of time to make parent contact. Being friendly and real to at risk students paid dividends. The students came to school and interacted with the teachers and I rarely had to call home. Once they realized that I cared for them they began to work for A's. I used my extra time to take some video correspondence courses while at work. Together with some summer classes I had started in 1987 I moved from M.A. to M.A. + 15 on the salary schedule.

In the summer of 1980, Neil Padgett came back to driver education. His venture into insurance was not as profitable as he thought. He still sold insurance but only as a secondary job. Since I had run the program for the past three years he treated me as an equal. We would have between 100 to 120 students each summer and sometimes we would each teach a class. We usually had two other instructors who just did driving and no classroom. On two separate summers, I asked a colleague from Davenport to drive during the summer. Both of them completed the summer session but neither one ever drove again. They each had some difficult situations on the road. That is when I discovered that driver education is not good for everybody. You have to have some nerves of steel. I always let the student make their own driving decisions and I did not "ride" the instructor brake as some instructors did. I only used my brake to avoid a collision; otherwise I let the student run the red light as a learning experience. My experience told me that if I went to the brake, the student would also and think that they stopped the car instead of me. I never had a problem with student drivers although other drivers ran into us three different times, usually while we were stopped.

In 1983 the DeWitt school district decided to drop the driver education class from the school year curriculum. Neil asked if I would come to the school board meeting and put in a good word for the program and try to convince the board not to cut the program. Neil told me to come around 8:00 p.m. and I would be called to speak about 9:00 p.m. I sat there until 2:00 a.m. before they called me in to speak. I was done in ten minutes and I went home to a brief night's sleep before the start of the school day. The board decided to drop the program. I'm sure this was already decided before I came there. Neil was going to lose his job. Neil had was the state 2A basketball championship in 1981 and was well known in DeWitt. The school board would allow him to continue to teach in the high school and keep his basketball-coaching job if he would get special education certification. Neil did this and kept his job at the school until his retirement. I did not like the way this was handled and think there was some vendetta against Neil. The summer driver education program did not change and would continue as before.

By 1980 I was an established coach at Williams Junior High. Schedules varied from year to year but in 1981 Don Stroud was the 7th and 8th grade coach and we had identical schedules, so we practiced together. I had good relations with all of the wrestlers. After all, I had recruited most of them. Don was a laid-back kind of guy who lived in the past. He was always talking about teams he had in the past and putting down his current team. I always led the calisthenics at the beginning of practice and did every exercise I ever asked the kids to do, including wrestling. If we ran the halls or stairs I also led the way. I demonstrated all of the wrestling moves and did a lot of one on one with each wrestler. Don did not like my leadership. He was not an active coach. He did not want his team to learn some of the advanced moves I was working on. While I worked on gramby rolls with my team, he pulled his team off to the side for a little meeting. No wonder the 8th graders looked to me and not to their own coach. Don quit coaching wrestling after that, probably because of me.

In 1982 the principal could not find a wrestling coach to take the 7th and 8th grade team. I told him that I would coach both teams for both coaching salaries. He agreed. When the schedule was back to back I would coach from early November to mid-March. What a long haul that was. Some years the schedule was identical. In those years, I coached seventy wrestlers all at once. I started with fifteen wrestlers and a poor reputation to over seventy with championship capability. Overall, things paid off. From one city champion in 1978 to a championship team in 1984 was a good reward. We repeated in 1985 and in dual meets we defeated both Bettendorf and Wood Junior High. Bettendorf High School had recently been the state champions and they had an excellent feeder system. They almost always won. Wood had dominated Williams for years. Their coach Mike Voyles and I had a rivalry but we were soon to become friends.

In 1985 North High School opened with Eric Jobgen named as the head varsity coach. Eric had been the longtime assistant at West High School. Eric had asked Mike Voyles to be his assistant but he still needed a third coach. Eric called me to be the third man on his staff. This was a tough choice for me. I had developed a powerhouse at Williams and the next 9th grade team was going to be the city champions in 1986. It was a tough choice but I decided to leave Williams to coach at North. I would still teach at Williams but I was hoping that by coaching at North I might be able to get a teaching job there. Two years later that came true. Once on his staff, Eric told me that he offered me the job to cut the connection between Williams and West. I had been sending numerous wrestlers to West and Williams was an important feeder school. Eric hoped to cut that connection by removing me from the equation. It apparently worked. Williams won the 1986 championship but then drifted back to be an average team. Eric also needed someone who knew the wrestling rules. As a referee, I knew the rules inside and out and I helped him in this, as he was a weak in knowing all the rules.

So, in 1985 North became the newest 3A wrestling team. In Iowa, the forty-eight largest schools were in the 3A districts. Usually these were the schools with over 1000 students; although today those numbers are lower. North did not have a true wrestling room. It was a small gymnasium with side mats and a thirty-foot ceiling. There was no heater in the room and the winter temperatures were usually only in the 50's Fahrenheit. I had left the best junior high wrestling room for the worst high school room. That year I ran all of the pre-season workouts since Eric and Mike both coached football. I got to know most of the wrestlers before the season began. However, once the season began I found myself in a lesser roll. It's one thing to run practice with seventy wrestlers all by yourself and to be number three on a staff of three with twenty-five wrestlers. Eric was a hands-on coach. He is one I would call a technician. He had forgotten more wrestling than I had ever known. When he taught a wrestling move he went into so much depth that it took half an hour to watch the demonstration. Then when everyone went to practice it, he would stop everyone if one person couldn't do it right. This was not my style but I learned from it. My role became helping wrestlers one at a time. Sometimes I would wrestle them to help improve their skills. By doing this I had a number of wrestlers that looked to me for advice. Mike Voyles, on the other hand, mostly sat along the wall and blew the whistle. He was in charge of statistics and knowing about our opponents across the state. He knew a lot of people and had more time than anyone else because as the business teacher he only taught three classes.

The North wrestling team won about half of their meets throughout the Eric Jobgen years. We also had two or three wrestlers place in the state tournament every year. However, there was a slow decline in the number of wrestlers every year and many of them didn't have any wrestling skills. Eric had a tendency to just work with the best wrestlers and ignore the others. He usually picked the team for each meet and rarely had a wrestle off. That's where I came in. I could see that these wrestlers were losing heart and I tried to help. I disapprove of this type of coaching but I was loyal to Eric and stayed out of his way. On two separate occasions Eric got mad about something in the middle of practice and stormed out of the room. Mike and I just stood there not knowing what to do. Eric had left the building and went home. Mike and I would finish the practice session but we weren't sure what was happening. Fortunately, this was isolated but Eric never spoke about it. My role at North was very easy but required more time than when I was coaching junior high.

I had started out as a wrestling referee in 1974. I refereed for free at some elementary school intramurals and the little kid's tournaments that were sprouting up across the state. By 1980 I was working varsity meets for the MAC conference. That is the Mississippi Athletic Conference in southeast Iowa. I soon was working some Saturday tournaments and was developing a reputation for fairness. I couldn't get enough referee jobs to satisfy my desire. Certainly, I could use the money but something drives someone to perfection. I had set a goal for myself to referee in the state tournament before 1990. I needed more meets to referee so I got licensed in Illinois and applied to referee in the Mississippi Valley League. I even took the college wrestling exam and landed a tournament at Monmouth College that I did for several years. One night I refereed Iowa City West vs. Cedar Rapids Washington. When the meet was over a man rushed up to me wanting to know who I was. I told him my name and where I was from and he said he had never seen a wrestling match called so well. I thanked him but I don't know if I ever got more meets after that. His name was Clyde Bean and he was the coach of Iowa City High School. I only refereed a couple times in Illinois and I think my Iowa address was responsible for that.

In 1985 when I started coaching at North I gave up my MAC referee contracts but added local junior high meets to my schedule. My ties to a 3A school hindered my getting contracts and I began doing fewer meets each year. I was not known enough because I could not referee enough. I never reached my goal of working at the state tournament. That didn't matter, as more important things were about to overtake my life.

In the 1980's my family grew up. We had changed churches and now went to Grace Lutheran Church. Dan and Becky would get confirmed and I even was on the church council one year. However, we did have a bad experience. In 1981 five-year-old Becky was diagnosed with leukemia. Bonnie and I were devastated. Becky had been complaining that her legs hurt but we could see no reason for this. When the doctor examined her, he sent her to the University of Iowa Hospital and Clinics in Iowa City. This is where the children's hospital experts are. I spent the first night in Iowa City sleeping on the floor beside her bed. There was no Ronald McDonald House in those days. I looked up leukemia in the encyclopedia that was written in 1971 only to find that it said there was no cure. She took radiation treatments and lost all of her beautiful straight red hair. Eventually she came home and her hair grew back curly. She returned to school and we took her to Iowa City every year for checkups. When she turned eighteen the doctor declared her cured and she has never had a recurrence. We watched her play softball and volleyball through junior high and she was becoming quite the athlete.

Dan first played baseball when he was seven. He didn't do well as he was too young and couldn't concentrate on the game. In junior high he played football and then played on the football team when he went to North High in 1988. He played in the band and also did some show choir. He also took on a paper route when he was in junior high. I bought him a moped to use to deliver papers. When he had conflicts, I became his substitute. Becky took over his paper route when he went to high school and again I was the substitute.

Obviously, I encouraged my kids to go out for sports and other school activities. I did not let Josh start sports too early. He started wrestling when he was about seven. Then I had him sign up for a coed softball league before playing baseball. An interesting thing occurred on that softball team. I volunteered to help the coach during practice, which he appreciated. In the middle of the season he asked me if I would coach the team while he took his family on a week-long vacation. I agreed and we had a good week, then two weeks. In fact, he never came back and I finished the season for the team. Josh went on to play baseball right through his senior year of high school. He didn't always have the best coaches in Little League baseball. One coach he had was hated by almost everyone. Following a game that the team lost he held a team meeting and just chewed out everybody. When the team left, every one of the boys was crying. This is no way to treat nine-year-olds and just reinforced my bias toward bad coaching.

The church league softball team was not the only team I coached. In 1981, I had befriended one of my wrestlers and a student in my history class named Paul Wells. Paul even became a Civil War reenactor and went with me to several reenactments. His father, also named Paul Wells, called me one day in the spring of 1981. He told me how he appreciated how I coached and wondered if I could help him with a colt league team. He was the sponsor and head coach for a team and needed more help. He already had three other coaches but they often had conflicts with some of the game nights. I told him I played in a softball league but would help when I could. That summer I helped while also playing softball as well as doing driver education.

The next year Paul asked me to help again. Only this time I got no help and Paul senior was not around. I had to give up playing softball and some games didn't get over until midnight. I had to be the last one to leave and turn the lights out. Then I had to be up by 5:30 a.m. to get to driver education on time. That was a rough summer. I enjoyed the coaching and I was an aggressive coach. I recruited a number of wrestlers from my junior high team and they would do anything I said. Wrestlers have to be willing to take a risk. Once on a steal home play, my runner came running fast while the batter took a swing at the ball. The batter was called out because the umpire said it was not a pitch but a throw to the catcher and the runner was tagged out. I was hot about this call. Seldom have I ever gotten upset as a coach. I lost the argument and we went on, but it reminded me of how an umpire can affect the lives of young athletes. After the season, I gave up both baseball coaching and playing softball. I was more interested in my hobby of Civil War reenacting and my own children's games and I just didn't have enough time.

By 1981 my wife and children all had period Civil War clothing. We had our own modern tent where every slept but we spent the day partaking in old time games, cotillions, ladies' tea and battle reenactment. All of my children brought friends with them and we put them all into uniforms or dresses. About twelve times a year we loaded up the family in the station wagon and spent a weekend at various locations throughout the Midwest. We all enjoyed it and even went to the 125th anniversary of the Battle of Gettysburg in Pennsylvania in 1988. By then we had gotten rid of the modern tent and had two authentic tents.

Earl Monholland had left the unit that he formed in 1980. We were seven reenactors without a leader. I took over the registrations for our unit and I soon had recruited several newer recruits. We were family oriented and there were a lot of kids in our camp. I was eventually elected by the group to take command and I took on the rank of a lieutenant. We then got together and decided we needed a proper name. After looking through historical records we decided to be Scott's Tennessee Battery. That's all there is to it. There is no vast national organization of Civil War reenactors. In 1985, we incorporated our unit as a 501 c (3) not for profit corporation in the state of Iowa. Also, our numbers had grown to more than twenty active adult men.

We still had the three steel mortars but Dave Wizer, who was in the Coast Guard, built a mountain howitzer at the Rock Island Arsenal workshop. Then Ed Reiter bought another mountain howitzer. In 1986, we began the construction of a carriage for an original 3-inch ordnance rifle. Everyone in our group spent the winter to help build the carriage and it was ready for the 125th anniversary of the Battle of Shiloh. Mike

Cunningham joined us that year and he already had a reproduction 3-inch ordnance rifle. By the end of the decade we owned nine Civil War artillery pieces. I was a part owner of a brass coehorn mortar with Dennis Anderson and Gene Jorandby had built a five-inch mortar and we had over one hundred people belong to our group at one time or another.

There is one more thing. In the fall of 1980 I read a local newspaper article about a Revolutionary War reeenactor that lived in Bettendorf. I called him on the phone and he invited me to his house. His name was Gregory Crawford and he belonged to the 84th Highland Regiment, a British Army unit formed in Nova Scotia. That very day I accepted the shilling, actually a quarter. I of course called Boyd Ayres and we were both in the British Army. I attended Revolutionary War reenactments for about three years and then gave it up. I could not do justice by doing two types of reenacting. However, I did have an experience of a lifetime in October of 1981. Boyd and I were allowed to take three days off from school with pay to attend the 200th anniversary of the Battle of Yorktown. We agreed to put on a presentation after we returned. We were never asked to do the presentation but Boyd and I dressed up in our uniforms once a year to give a presentation to our classes.

The 1980's was a good time to live in the Midwest. The Kindig family was achieving in many ways under my paternal leadership. Every year my salary increased and we achieved many goals. We had started a family hobby in reenacting and all of the children were playing in sports. Becky had survived a difficult illness and it appeared that we all had made the right choices in life. I didn't like the debt that I had accrued but it was manageable and the best decade of the twentieth century was on the horizon.

CHAPTER 7

The 1990's

Pursuit of Goals

In March of 1990 North High School had its annual winter sports banquet. Following a guest speaker and a potluck supper each sport went to different rooms to present awards to the winter teams. The wrestling team had dwindled to only seventeen athletes and several of them were seniors. After the awards were given out and the athletes and their parents had gone home, Eric Jobgen told Mike Voyles and myself that he would not be returning next season as the varsity wrestling coach. Although I didn't see this coming, I was not surprised. Eric had been cut from the teaching staff at North High and was going to be a Physical Education teacher at Buchanan Elementary School. He had lost the confidence of the administration and he was somewhat depressed at the current situation.

Mike Voyles and I both applied for the varsity coach position. We also had a new principal, Jim Andrews, coming to North High and ultimately, he would make the decision. We both had separate interviews and during the summer I was informed that I would be the new varsity coach. I asked Mike to stay as my assistant and he agreed. I then went looking for a third coach. Mike Wood, who had worked with me back in my days at Smart, asked to be hired for the job. He was currently coaching the 9th grade wrestling team at Sudlow Junior High School. He also was going to have his two sons attending North and they were wrestlers. I knew Mike Wood and I didn't think he would offer any benefits to me. I inquired about a young man, Jesse Lira, who was the 7th and 8th grade coach at Sudlow. I even asked Mike Wood what he thought of Jesse. He gave me a good recommendation and I hired Jesse after his interview.

Jesse Lira was only about twenty-two years old, married with two children, soon to be three, and a former wrestler from West High School. Jesse worked at a local licorice factory and was taking classes at St. Ambrose University in Davenport. Jesse was born in Mexico and had his green card. He also was serving in the Iowa National Guard and would be called up for Operation Desert Storm. Needless to say, Jesse became one of my best friends and confidant, a relationship I still maintain.

Also in the spring of 1990 there was a change in my teaching assignment. The school board was cracking down on principals who had teachers teaching classes that they were not qualified to teach. The Social

Studies department head came to me to say that I would be teaching Early Western Civilization and Modern U.S. History for the next school year. I was elated. Finally, I was going to teach in the field that I had gotten a master's degree. I still had the Student Senate as well.

I was forty-one years old and had reached all of the goals in life that I had set years ago. I still read twenty-five books a year. Usually more than that and most of them were in the areas of history that I taught classes in. I had attained a Master's degree in history and written a book on the French and Indian War. I had established a family and moved into a large two-story home. My career had attained exactly what I wanted, teaching high school history. I had taken an interest in wrestling to a point where I became a 3A wrestling coach. If only my old coach, Keith Young, could see me now. I met Beets Dotson in 1993 in Cleveland, Ohio during the National Wrestling tournament. He was then coaching at the University of New Mexico. After I told him who I was he seemed puzzled. I don't think he remembered me. I am sure that his brother-in-law, Franc Freeman, the coach from Bettendorf, explained things to him later. He was also there at the time.

It was now time to set some new goals in my life. I had put away about $12,000 for my children's education and it was time to put some money aside for retirement. I got an agent and set up a 403 (b) plan. My goal of refereeing at the Iowa State Wrestling Tournament was no longer attainable. Instead I set a goal to have a state champion come from my wrestling room. I also wanted to be known more for my teaching than for my coaching. I was a mature teacher/coach with nineteen years of experience in the prime of life.

The 1990's were a good financial time. It was the time of the peace dividend and the economy improved throughout the decade. My salary grew from $40,000 to $50,000 a year with driver education increasing to $18.00 an hour. In 1990 the teacher's union sued the school board on the grounds that all of the teachers taught six classes instead of the usual five classes and a supervision period. This could have been a $10,000 windfall for me except for one thing. The school district did not consider my student government class to be a class. The union did not fight for me and I missed out on what every other teacher at North High received. However, my teaching assignment now had four history classes, the student government class and a supervision period. The union let me down again. I continued to teach DIPs class on Saturday's and worked the homework hotline twice a week until this job ended in 1995.

With all of the good economic times there was one thing I did not expect. In the summer of 1996 I still felt that I had my finances under control. I carried about $5,000 of debt on my credit card and had never missed a payment on anything. A few years before Bonnie had gone to Kaplan University to improve her career. She became a travel agent and we took a couple of trips at discount prices. At work, she made new friends and went out with them after work. That summer day in 1996 she handed me all of her credit card bills. She could not pay them and they totaled over $50,000. She also wanted a separation from our marriage. We divorced the next year and I agreed to pay all of her debts if she agreed to give me the house. Our divorce was uncontested but I could not pay of the debts. In 1997, I filed for bankruptcy. This allowed me to start over. I kept my house and one car and I had all the debts erased. My income remained the same. By the end of the decade I was financially stable with my goals still intact.

My career at North now put me in the limelight. I was teaching what I always wanted to teach and I was meeting some people with new ideas. Bruce Buffe was the supervisor for the homework hotline as well as the English coordinator at the local Education Agency. He wanted to know if I would try some new teaching techniques. He even offered to pay a $200.00 stipend each time I tried something. The way this worked was that I would try a new technique in one class and have another class do nothing and serve as the control group. It didn't take long for me to see that the new technique was raising student grades and this was not fair to the control group. I soon had a reputation for innovation and as the word spread more students wanted to be in my classes. Fair, firm and friendly paid dividends again.

In 1998 Dave Swim came to my room with an opportunity. He was only fifty-eight and was retiring at the end of the year. He wanted me to be the new department head for social studies. Dave was burned out with teaching and frankly was not doing well. I was going ahead of several members of the staff who had more seniority than I did. I accepted and the principal approved. I moved to a new classroom that had a separate office. I now had to attend administrative meetings both at our school but also four times a year at the district administrative office. I had more responsibility but also got additional pay.

In the 1990s the driver education job I had at DeWitt continued with no changes. We were running from 120 to 150 students each summer and many summers there were six instructors needed. In 1999 the school district decided to drop the driver education program completely. The replacement program would be run by the AEA with Neil and myself designated as the lead instructors. Nothing changed in regards to the program except that I got my paycheck from someone else.

When I took over the wrestling program in 1990 it was at rock bottom. Some wrestlers stayed with the program when they found out that I was the coach. Parents told me that their boy would have quit if Jobgen had stayed. I now had new duties and went about the job of improving the program. Financially the program had few funds. The school district only allowed $400 for my use in the program and that would be needed for new uniforms and headgear. It would take several years to raise enough money. I decided to raise the money we needed ourselves and I would involve the team to do this. First, we held a car wash. Dave Macias was a parent of one of the wrestlers and owned a Rudy's Tacos restaurant. He offered his facility and I brought the team and the cheerleaders to wash cars. I also sold ads for a poster that we gave out free and put them in some of the stores. We did this every year.

We had a wrestling club for elementary school age kids that I now took over. During the wrestling season the club met from 6:30 p.m. to 7:30 p.m. on Monday and Wednesday evenings. We broke up into age groups and I had the wrestling team teach their own group of wrestlers. We charged the kids $5 but gave them a T-shirt and an entry into our tournament. All of my wrestlers also got T-shirts. We were very successful and had 40-50 kids each night. Our wrestling tournament took place between Christmas and New Year's. The entry fee was $5 and we often had almost 1000 wrestlers.

The tournament ran from 7:00 a.m. until evening. I got wrestling gear from USA Wrestling and sold it for a 25% cut and we sold our own gator aid. We made over $5000 in one day that was turned right back into the team. Of course, I needed a lot of volunteers to make this work. The wrestlers were the referees and the parents were scorekeepers, timers and worked the tables. Several mothers filled out our brackets and tallied the wins and losses. I solely was responsible for this operation with Mike Voyles and Jesse Lira taking charge of mats or books. I solved problems and had to deal with the unruly parents.

So how did I intend to rebuild the wrestling team? I went back to the basics and treated everyone fairly. I never would pick the team and anyone could challenge for any spot. Once we were wrestling with some modest skills I would work on endurance. A wrestler needs to have enough energy to wrestle for six minutes without a rest period. To accomplish this, we would wrestle none stop with only small breaks until the team was exhausted. Then we took a break and I would give a pep talk. Then back at it. As the years went on this technique paid off. I began to add more advanced moves and I took the team to summer wrestling camps. My favorite was at the University of Nebraska in Lincoln. I took about ten wrestlers there where we got instruction in wrestling techniques and some hard wrestling with our team against other teams from all over the country. We would wrestle four or five times a day and nobody ever got hurt.

I had my assistants but I needed some people to help with tasks that coaches just don't have time for like folding clothing and sorting equipment. For this I always needed some student manager. Every year I had more volunteers than I could use. I usually took some girls for this job and they were considered part of the team. One of the jobs was to learn how to keep score and this was a big responsibility. That first year my son Dan was a manager. Being the coach's son he also got drafted to wrestle a time a two.

In the first year the wrestling team had only one victory and we were forfeiting four weights. I built a good camaraderie with the team and we worked on the skills for each wrestler. Mike Voyles took his usual role of knowing the competition but in the practice room he usually blew the whistle while Jesse and I worked with the wrestlers. On the team bench he tried to control the matches and his information he gave me was not useful. I began to think he was just making things up and I soon gave up his council. Jesse Lira, on the other hand, was very professional and I soon realized I could count on him. We qualified two wrestlers for the state tournament and they were both juniors. Tony Bibbs, whose father was the wrestling coach at Central High School, had an excellent season but did not place in the tournament. Manuel Macias, however, made it to the finals. He had pulled some muscles in a tournament back in January and had been out of the lineup until the district tournament. He was now wrestling against Derek Monsieur from Newton. Manuel was behind 4-1 at the start of the 3rd period. Mike Voyles told me he should take the down position to try for a reversal but Manuel had already been rode out for a period. I rejected this idea and told Manuel to take the top position and turn his opponent. He rode Monsieur very hard and was awarded stalling points twice but ran out of time and lost 4-3. There should have been another stalling call but this match was in the hands of the referee. I had made the right decision knowing Manuel's strength. I almost achieved my coaching goal in the first season.

In the second year Manuel and Tony led the team and I was busy recruiting in my classroom. We had a full team and a very tough schedule. I soon had my first victory over Bettendorf when I made a quick lineup change to my benefit. Franc Freeman knew I had outfoxed him and I became an equal of coaches in his eyes. The team finished in the middle of the MAC conference and our victory over West High School made North the top school in Davenport. My daughter Becky became a team manager and this helped a lot. Dan had graduated in 1991 and Becky would graduate in 1994.

I worked hard to make two changes to wrestling in Davenport. First, I wanted the 9th grade wrestlers to be eligible to wrestle at the high school level. Davenport was one of the few school districts that did not have 9th grade in their high schools. The feeder schools were not sending as many wrestlers to the high school and I wanted an extra year to develop the athletes. In 1994 the school board finally approved the addition of 9th grade to the high schools, just in time for my son Josh when he arrived at North.

The second thing was to have a new wrestling room built at our school. With the passage of a one-cent sales tax for school improvements North was going to have a new gymnasium built in 1995. I attended several of the parent/administration meetings to lobby for a new wrestling room. With wrestling parents backing me and with the principal's support we had the blue prints presented with a new locker room and weight room adjacent to the wrestling room. I also had enough money for a new wrestling mat at about $9,000. I ordered a one-piece 38X38 foot mat that would fit perfectly in the new practice room. Several months later I found out that the principal cut out the wrestling room. He had intended to do this all along but did not want to tell parents what he was doing. He lied to me and I could never forgive him for such a heartbreak. When the new mat arrived, it could not fit into our old practice room and had to stay rolled up on the gym floor. It could only be used for home meets.

In the Christmas break of 1993 I had a rare opportunity to go to Florida. My father had retired in 1983 and sold my boyhood home. Then my parents built a small house on a lake in Minnesota so dad could enjoy fishing in his retirement. In the winter, they moved south. They were living in Florida and wanted to take all of the grandchildren to Disney World. With Dan still at home going to community college, Becky in high school and Josh in junior high, the time was perfect. I had never missed a wrestling practice in twenty years. Mike Voyles assured me that he could run the practices and I went to Florida. When I returned home the phone was ringing off the wall. There were some problems in the wrestling room. Mike Voyles had pulled the authority card on the wrestlers and had kicked some wresters off the team. Parents were mad as hell and I had a problem to solve. The short of it is that I restored the wrestlers to the team and had to deal with Mike. He stayed on the rest of the season but it was his last with me. How many times in life have I seen a coach ruin a young man's life? Here it was again and on my watch. I have devoted my life to fairness and giving everyone a chance and I have seen good results.

The next season Jesse became my assistant and I needed a new coach. Mike Wood was still interested but I already had to deal with a coach with a big ego. Instead I selected a young nineteen-year-old Bob McClellan. Bob may have been too close in age to the wrestlers but he had heart. I thought I could mold him into my team but he pretended to be the head coach when he should have hung back. He was not a good choice but I kept him for three seasons and then let him go. One year I had a volunteer coach. His name was Jim Olsen and he was a pastor at a Baptist church near Blue Grass, Iowa. He was close to my age and was a great addition to my team. One time he told me that he had never seen anyone inspire a team as well as I did. In practice, after the first thirty minutes of unlimited takedowns I always held a brief pep talk before we worked on technique. Jim told me it was during this time that I convinced everyone about the power of confidence and self-esteem. Jim only stayed one year and then volunteered at West High because his son was going there.

The 1996-97 wrestling season was the best yet. We finally had a winning season and did it big with only five losses. There were twenty-one freshman on the team and I had over forty wrestlers in practice. We did well in the tournaments and took six wrestlers to the state tournament. Two of them, Dominick Carter and Nick Ulloa took 6th place but they could have done better. I had taken from two to six wrestlers to the state tournament since I became the varsity coach. It looks like I had finally turned North High School into league power.

The next year turned out to be my last year of coaching. I had every reason to believe that this would be my best year ever. From the beginning, everything started to go wrong. First several very good seniors decided not come out for the team. Nam Ngyuen, a good friend of my son, was ranked number three in the state in the Des Moines Register preseason poll at 103 pounds. Andy Robinson, who wrestled at 171 pounds decided to concentrate on his singing. He did place in the state chorus competition but I believe he would have placed at state wrestling too. There were only three new freshman on the wrestling team that year and of the twenty-one freshman the year before only seven came out in 1997. Something had happened in the 8th grade-wrestling program as the numbers were drying up.

So, we started the 1997 season with decreased numbers but still had some good athletes. My son Josh was a senior and had winning records since his freshman year, breaking into the varsity lineup at mid-season. He had defeated many opponents this season when he had to be pulled from the lineup because of an injury. It turned out to be a hernia and his wrestling was over. A friend of his, Leroy Nimmers, was having a great year but he had girlfriend problems and began skipping practice. He could beat everyone in the MAC but blew his match in the district tournament by having no energy. He apparently had other things on his mind. Ben Becker was an aspiring junior whose last match he wrestled for me summed up his bad performance. To go to the state tournament he needed a takedown to win. In the third period he chose neutral and had two minutes to score. After the two minutes he had only pushed his opponent around and never took a shot. I asked him, "Why didn't you shoot.?" He responded, "I needed more time." Two special mentions were Tony Cole and Brian Zirkel. In our meet against Dubuque Senior High School they both pinned their opponents with a spladel. This is a complex move we worked on and they perfected it. The Dubuque coaches gave me quite the compliment on these two plus the ability to actually do the move. I gave Tony a ride to school every morning to do a morning practice. Instead he found a place to take a nap. He didn't have the desire to be a champion. Brian was good but not consistent but he had the skills to win, if he would use them.

I had my hands full with these athletes but I also saw the coaches in the MAC begin to turn on me. At seeding meetings if there were any disagreements they would be handled with coach's agreements or even a vote. I had another winning season in 1997-98 and dominated some of these teams for the first time. I could usually expect Davenport Central and West to side with me, but not this year. North Scott was a close ally of mine, but not this year. Finally I thought Dubuque Senior was my newest friend and we had talked about sticking together, but not this year. None of my wrestlers got a break in the district seeding and because of the lack of energy this was the first time in North history that no one qualified for the state tournament.

Jesse had predicted that I would retire from coaching as we went through the season. We talked about it from time to time not believing the changes that we were seeing. We had some crybabies on the team that hid when they could to avoid wrestling. Of course the better wrestlers would then pick on them and they would come crying to a coach. At the end of the season there was only seven returning underclassmen. I had done everything I could and had built up a great team only to have it come apart on me. For the past eight years I had put in fourteen hours a day for four months and six days a week. I was tired. After twenty-six years of wrestling I resigned my coaching job in April 1998. But old wrestlers never die they just wrestle in a different way. I became a Hawkeye fan. I bought season tickets to the University of Iowa wrestling.

I wanted to make sure that the North wrestling team had a good coach. I personally picked Steve Medina to replace me. Steve was following right behind me as he was the wrestling coach at Williams and had some good teams. I met with Steve, Dave Macias and a few parents to explain everything that I did as a head coach. There was $5000 in the kid's club treasury and the school had accumulated two years of coaching money. It was all in writing and he could call on me if he needed help or advise. He never called. In fact he never finished his first season as he had health issues that caused him to resign in mid-season. In the next six seasons there would be six different coaches. North never returned to the days of the good teams.

My children all came of age in the 1990s. Dan graduated from high school in 1991 and went to Scott Community College. He had several jobs when he was in high school but what he liked best was the job he got when he was eighteen. He was a Pizza delivery driver. He liked to drive and liked to be up late at night. Eventually he dropped out of college and he got promoted to assistant manager at the Papa John store on Brady Street. This led him to become the manager of the store. This store did so well that he was transferred to the new store opening in Ames, Iowa. After he got that store running he was transferred to a Papa John store in Cedar Rapids that had poor sales. He turned that store around in a few months. He had found his niche being successful selling pizza.

Becky graduated in 1994 and enrolled at the University of Northern Iowa. She was in the marching band but didn't take her studies seriously and dropped out. Working some part time jobs back in Davenport she met James Bailey. They were married in 1997 and my first grandchild, Kaitlyn Victoria Bailey was born in 1999.

Josh was confirmed at Grace Lutheran Church and graduated from high school in 1997. He then went to the University of Iowa. He dropped out after the first semester because of bad grades but continued to live in Iowa City. He tried several jobs until his brother got him into Papa Johns in Cedar Rapids. At the age of twenty-one he was already a store manager.

All three of my children used the money I had saved for them to go to school but it would never have been enough to go for four years. Today they own homes and all live in Davenport. Dan got married in 2005 and has two children, Madelyn and Logan. Becky had a son Colton and a stepson Sumner. Josh got married in 2006 and has three children, Lukas, Hannah and Olivia.

My marriage with Bonnie ended in divorce in May 1997. She had moved out of our house on one of those long Saturday wrestling meets I was at. I returned home that night to some empty rooms but she wanted to be happy, so I let her go. I still had Josh at home as I would be responsible for him until he graduated from high school. I had no other interests and was not seeing anyone. One evening in June 1997 I had a phone number for a person named Connie Stewart. She was recently divorced and I gave her a call. A few days later I met her for coffee at the St. Ambrose Bookstore and Coffee Shop. She fell in love with me first but I was a little slow because of what I had just gown through. Her interests were exactly the same as mine and marriage was in the air. We waited until Becky had her wedding and then we were married on September 4, 1997. The wedding was held in my backyard and Dan had Papa John's deliver pizza for our guests. This was a Thursday evening and we went to work the next day. Sometimes I think many people marry too young. This was not true to me but it probably applied to Bonnie. People have a better idea of what to expect when they marry later in life.

I told Connie before we got married that I was a Civil War reenactor and she had to accept me being gone on some weekends. She asked what side I was on and I told her the south. She was pleased as she was born in South Carolina. In fact she went to every reenactment in the summer of 1998 including the 135th Anniversary of the Battle of Gettysburg. She portrayed Pvt. John O'Farrell but she also put on a very pretty ball gown as Mrs. Marsh.

I hesitated about getting married without a firm understanding of our finances. Connie was the department head of nursing at the Good Samaritan Nursing facility and had her own paychecks. Her ex-husband was making the payments on her car. I had my own paychecks and we determined to split the bills with each of us responsible for certain ones. After a few months her ex-husband stopped paying for her car. I could not help as I was still dealing with Bonnie's debts. The car was repossessed and Connie was forced into bankruptcy. It wasn't long after that and I went into bankruptcy as well.

In 1990 Scott's Battery had become a very authentic reenactment group and we had a reputation for safety as well as precision in drill. We were also asked to put on the annual Civil War Muster at the Village of East Davenport. This was the largest reenactment in Iowa at the time. With a budget of over $20,000 I was now in charge of all of the activities at this annual festival. I could rely on some twenty-five men and their families to help us run registration, contests, ladies' activities and the ball. We ran this event until 1994 when it was moved to Scott County Park. The event finally ended in 1997.

In 1992 I went to Usher's Ferry in Cedar Rapids to set up a cannon display. I met with Vicki Hughes and we agreed to put on a Civil War muster there next year. I was now putting on two Civil War events every year. Just like the kid's wrestling tournament, I had to do all the prearrangements and send out mailings to all prospective participants. There was no internet in those days. We stopped having this event in 2003.

Civil War reenacting was my escape from the modern world. The people I camped with were my friends and helped me during my divorce. I soon was known in the state of Iowa to be a Civil War reenactment promoter. I set up several more events but most of them were just one-time events. I also recruited many of the members of Scott's Battery and they are all upstanding people.

The 1990s were a very good time to have money invested and my portfolio grew in spite of my bankruptcy. In fact the laws of bankruptcy in the United States were very favorable. Sometime in late 1999 the gross income of my entire life passed the one-million-dollar mark. This truly was a good time to be alive and I don't regret any of the choices that were made during this time. I doubt that my grandfather could believe that such a thing could happen. So far, I have not compared myself to others except my own family. Your geographic place of birth and where you live are major factors. Also the amount of education and the willingness to sacrifice early in life can pay big dividends later in life. Then there are the choices people make in life. I choose to skip expensive and sometimes dangerous habits such as drinking and smoking. The choice to not ever take illegal drugs helps keep a clear head. Things like divorce and bankruptcy can be devastating. My children were already grown up so the effect on them was not as traumatic as it would be for small children and the bankruptcy courts actually eases the financial stresses as long as you don't repeat it.

This book can end here, as its focus is the late 20th century. I have shown how life in Iowa from the 1950's was a pretty good time to be born. I will continue into the 21st century since this is my autobiography and life will still be a good time to be alive. Others may say that life was not as good for the millennial that was born in the 1990s. If that is true, one must evaluate not just the time and place of birth but to the choices that people make in life. If the government interferes too often in your choices the outcomes may not be as favorable. Each generation must strive to do better than the previous one. Take responsibility for what you do and the path you decide to follow.

In the next chapter I will continue the story of my life. At the age of 51 I had achieved the height of my career and would need to prepare for retirement. Two stock market drops are in the next decade. What decisions will I make?

CHAPTER 8

The 2000's

Toward Retirement

In April of 2000 I put my house on Forest Rd. up for sale. I no longer needed a two-story four-bedroom home. The bedrooms were on the upper floor and the washing machine was in the basement. All of my children were grown and were living on their own and what I really needed was a retirement home. Connie and I started looking at homes as well as some condos. We soon realized what we needed was to build our own home. Our home sold in just thirty days and we had just thirty more days to move out.

I drew up plans for a two-bedroom ranch with a walkout basement. We found a model home built by Chuck Pekios and we admired the construction. So I hired Chuck to build our home in the Garner Farms edition of Davenport. It was located one mile from North High School and about two miles from Good Samaritan, where Connie worked. This was much closer to work than the Forest Road house and I would be able to walk to work. The house sold for $150,000 about $20,000 more than I expected. I benefited from a recent upturn in the housing market. Our new house would cost $172,000 and I had a six percent mortgage.

Since we had to be out of our house by the end of May and the new house would not be completed until August, we moved in with Connie's sister who was renting a farmhouse in rural Pleasant Valley. I had sold her my Mazda pickup truck when I filed for bankruptcy and she still owed me $1300.00. So she said this would make us even. This house was old and not in very good shape. I called it "green acres" after the television show of the same name. We had a mattress on the floor of the attic and lived out of our suitcases. I took a shower in the basement where I had to fight the cobwebs each time and operate the water flow with a pair of pliers.

In August we moved in about two weeks late and I began walking to school every day except for bad weather. I continued to do this for the rest of my career. By the summer of 2001 I began the construction for finishing the basement. I finished a large family room and a bedroom that same fall. The next year I added a bathroom and an unfinished game room. In the game room I built a 10 X 10-foot game table for the 2000 miniatures I had painted. About a dozen friends come over to play Johnny Reb III on my table several times a year. I did all of the work on this basement including the electrical and plumbing. In 2003 I refinanced the house with a 4-3/4 percent mortgage on a ten-year loan. I paid more than the minimum and paid the house off in seven years.

Following my bankruptcy, I never owed on a credit card again. In fact, I still used credit cards but paid off my balance every month and received rewards from the credit card company. Now I was making money using a credit card. It was also time to put the maximum each month into my 403 (b). When the stock market dropped in 2001 I changed my 403 (b) to another firm. I was getting no advice. I now had an annual sit down to discuss my finances. When the market dropped in 2008 I decided to stop my 403 (b) and put my future inputs into a Roth IRA that I had started in 2006. I also kept some CDs at the bank for emergencies. I would be prepared when I decided to retire.

My teaching salary continued to increase as did the driver education wages. By 2010 the teaching salary had topped $62,000 and driver ed. Paid $22.00 an hour. I sometimes bragged that I was the highest paid teacher in Davenport. I don't know if that was true but I was making over $80,000 a year in 2009. What a change since those early days of teaching in 1971.

Teaching school had gone through many phases in my career. I took courses in 1971 called Schools Without Failure and applied the ideas to my classroom. I also went through mini-courses, career education, positive practice, assertive discipline, being a mentor and many in-service lessons. I always tried everything. If it worked it became part of my repertoire, if it didn't I let it go. I was now the department head and had a good reputation in the school district. In 2001 North High School was going to make a further change to help improve student scores. We were going to start block scheduling.

I held a series of meeting with all of the social studies teachers at North. There were seven of us and a few special education teachers joined in. The typical class was about 55 minutes long. We were going for 90 minutes that is too long to do one teaching technique. The teacher lecture was to be abandoned. There were to be no period long films shown. We were going to get students involved in their learning with a more hands on approach. A teacher presentation would be no longer than fifteen minutes and often done with a power point presentation. Students would get involved in cooperative learning groups and project presentations. A video would be kept short and only used to support the topic being presented that day or the day before. The computer had come to the classroom in 1999 and the school now had computer labs for student use. Students would now support their learning with sources, and Google is not a source. I kept a supply of 30 X 40 inch posters for the department and we decided to use blue books for final exams and I made sure that we had these supplies. The rule was 30-30-30. Do something for 30 minutes and then do something else. We all agreed to work this way.

So why the big change? Student scores had been falling and student discipline was less than desirable. I had seen this coming and as the millennia's arrived it was only going to get worse. We also hired a consultant to come to our school several times a year to work with our school to be more successful. I soon found that many of the new ideas he brought to us I was already doing. I invited him to my classroom to see what I was doing. I also invited other teachers to come in and observe a session of my class, such as a cooperative learning exercise. No one ever came. I brought my concern to Betsy Fair, an assistant principal. I asked her why teachers were not at their doors during passing time and doing the required teacher duties. She shrugged me off and called me an anomaly.

During this decade I was having a student teacher every year and I was an evaluator for NCA. Every school has to be evaluated every ten years by NCA and I became a social studies evaluator. I had already done this unofficially with my own department and now I did it at schools I had never been in. To make a long story short let me just say that I saw a lot of bad teachers. I use the word bad but many of them could be trained. Don't think that there are only good teachers out there. I feel sorry for students who have "bad" teachers and their lack of learning or discipline may not be their fault. Some teachers never change. What worked in 1975 must still work today, right? These teachers do not want to work hard with new lessons because they think the old lesson is just fine. One teacher at North even had the students read the newspaper for thirty minutes while he read his emails. Another teacher took the class to the computer lab and then left them to go have coffee in faculty lounge.

I blame the union for this. It is almost impossible to fire a teacher and the students suffer. My own training back in college was not very good. I learned on the job. Some teachers are incompetent and stay in the classroom. Some come late to work and leave early with no repercussions. I knew a teacher that was fired for watching porn on his computer with students in the classroom. That was one of the few times where bad actions of a teacher were swiftly dealt with.

In 2007 the principal of our school, Jane Andrews, wanted me to spearhead a committee to look into a project to evaluate a student's employability. It involved taking the students grades, attendance and a criteria of good and bad characteristics and run them through a computer to present a score for employers to see when they want to hire high school students. I had never heard of such a thing before but with a committee of ten faculty members we worked on this for over three months. When I presented the findings to Jane she responded that we can't do this. Then why did you ask me to do it? This type of busy work did not make me happy. I would never trust a principal again.

The students of the twenty-first century still had many excellent scholars but more and more students were becoming unruly. In 2001 our school made an arrangement to offer college credit for certain courses. Since I had a M.A. degree in history I was the only faculty member who could teach a U.S. History to 1877 course. I became an adjunct professor with Scott Community College and taught the class in my classroom at North for several years. Eventually North added AP U.S. History and although I was fully qualified to teach this course I decided to let the newest member in the social studies department teach this class. I was headed in a different direction.

Those unruly students were failing classes and didn't seem to care. I had them in my class all of the time. First, we set up a class called credit recovery. I was one of several teachers who volunteered to teach this class. Here students would come to complete class work from the previous semester. With ten to fifteen students I juggled individual lessons and proctored the retake of their tests. Then we had retake classes. I volunteered for this class as I knew no one else in my department would do the right thing. First, I did 9th grade American Studies part one and then part two. I even volunteered for 10th grade history. Keep it simple and work the basics. Reading, writing and class participation with me on top of them the entire 90 minutes. I had a 98% success rate. Then we instituted a class for those scoring below the 20th percentile on national tests. Some of these students scored low because they just colored in the dots on the test and refused to try. Others really needed the help. I worked with another teacher and we divided the thirty students into three groups. One with me, one with him and the third on the computers working vocabulary and reading skills. We rotated the groups every thirty minutes. Times had changed since that first class in 1971 where I only had one F for the entire year.

In the summer of 2000 I returned to DeWitt to teach driver education as usual. However, some things had changed. The AEA had taken over the driver education program but the school still provided the classroom. I still did the same thing I always did but now I got my check from someone else. Another change was that Neil Padgett would not be with the program anymore. He had just retired from DeWitt and was going to try real estate. Unfortunately Neil died the next year. He was a heavy smoker his whole life and would rather smoke than eat. It had finally caught up with him at the age of 62. We had 150 students that summer with six instructors. I was doing all of the classroom again. The best thing about the AEA is that we always drove new cars. DeWitt had been using used cars for the past decade.

In 2003 we had completed another summer of driver education but we only had 90 students. I'm not sure why there was this drop, but the AEA had a contract to teach 150 students. Don Willardsen was the director of driver education at the AEA. In October he wanted to know if I would teach an after-school driver education program after school. I had just cashed in a bunch of CDs to buy a Civil War cannon and need some additional income. I said yes. I worked with one partner, Dan Dunn, and the two of us split the forty-two hours per week to complete each program. We did four that winter/spring and five each year after that. Dan was an elementary P.E. teacher in Davenport and we both had to make those drives to DeWitt just like we did in the summer. Dan became a close longtime friend.

In 2005 the Davenport Community School District dropped the driver education program from their curriculum. The AEA was going to take over the program. The new driver education supervisor was Anne Budde. I knew Anne going back to when she was a driver education student in DeWitt back in 1985. She had also been the athletic director at North just a few years before. She asked me if I would take over the driver education program at North. I said yes. I completed my last DeWitt driver education class in June, it was my 31st year. I started my driver education class at North in August, before school started.

I had now come full circle from being rejected in 1972 to teach driver education in Davenport to being head of the program in 2005. I taught the driver education in my classroom at North so I did not need to set up and tear down every class like I did in DeWitt. I also ran all of the after-school programs and I worked as many as seven sessions each year. I had some long days from 7:00 a.m. to 8:30 p.m. many days. I had taught forty-four sessions when I was at DeWitt over thirty-one years and I would teach thirty-five sessions in the next five years. Why did I want to do this? Retirement was near and any money made in driver education would boost my pension.

Anne Budde asked me to write the curriculum for the AEA driver education program. I did this and it is now used by dozens of schools in east central Iowa. At the request of Betsy Fair, I was also writing gold standard lesson plans for the North staff through our consultant. I was working as hard as ever both for my students and for other teachers.

In October 2009, my wife Connie passed out at home. She had been suffering from an earache but now she was hospitalized with pressure on the brain. She was sent to University of Iowa Hospitals and Clinics where she underwent brain surgery. She nearly died and was in intensive care for a week. She was in the hospital for six weeks and then spent three months in therapy. She lost her short-term memory and had to learn to walk again. She came home in March 2010 and needed daily care. At first, I saw her at night and weekends and when she got home and needed care I decided that I would retire from teaching. I had intended to retire the next year but now was the time. I had worked thirty-nine years and had only been sick three days. I took twenty days of sick time to help Connie that spring and found other people to help her the days I was not there. When I retired I gave back to the school district 565 unused sick days. I officially retired on 30 June 2010.

Throughout the early 2000s I continued to be a Civil War reenactor. I went to ten to twelve events each year including a few 145th anniversary national events. In 2003, I bought a cannon because we had more men coming to the events and we easily could man two guns. Connie no longer went along since she had back surgery in 2001.

In 2000, we took a guided trip to Italy. I had contacted the Educational Foundation and they offered a great trip to Italy for only $1500.00. I recruited students to go on the trip. I took about ten students on this trip and so I went for free. I wish I had done this kind of travel before. The students came back to school with a great experience. I used many of the things I learned on the trip in my Early Western Civilizations class and had many pictures and books to share. We made four more trips over the decade visiting Ireland, England, France and Greece. These were excellent experiences not just for me but for the students.

In 2007, we took an EF trip to Ireland. On the last day, we were encouraged to ride on a jaunting cart ride through the National Park near Killarney. Connie and I were on a one-horse cart with three other students when the horse bolted and ran into the cart ahead of us. I had jumped off the cart just before impact but Connie was thrown to the pavement. She suffered broken bones in her right wrist and left leg and was taken to the hospital in Tralee. I had two parents in my group and they agreed to make sure that my group made it back to the United States. Meanwhile, Connie and I would remain in Ireland for another ten days. The doctor would not release her until he was sure that she could travel. I had to arrange an ambulance ride to the airport as well as get plane tickets from a local travel agent. American insurance is not accepted in foreign countries. I had to pay over $20,000 to get home. Later my insurance company reimbursed me. After that we would never travel without travel insurance.

I continued to follow Iowa wrestling and Jesse Lira and I would travel together often for my favorite sport. North finally got a steady wrestling coach and he asked me to run the winter freshman-wrestling tournament. This is the same wrestling tournament I won when I was at Smart back in 1975. Now it was much bigger and I knew how to keep team scores and run a tournament. I would continue this until I retired.

The 2000s were my highest income years ever and by the end of 2010 I had grossed my second million dollars. Only this time some of those dollars were now invested for my retirement. I loved teaching and had become a top veteran teacher. I didn't like to see the "dumbing" down of the curriculum or the teachers that didn't care. It was bad enough that so many students didn't care. I always took care of my own problems in the classroom and the distrust I had for principals meant I was on my own. There was now more paper work and more demands on my time. I was ready to retire. This is exactly why this was a good time to live. I did not have to work until I died like my great grandfather George Kindig. I not only had a pension, but I lived in a time when money increased with time and I had many vehicles in which to invest my money.

EPILOGUE

Beyond 2010

Retirement

Connie's therapy ended in November of 2010 but she still needed to continue physical activity. I took it upon myself to walk with her every day. We became mall walkers and continue to do this even today. In addition to walking with Connie I also walked the neighborhood about three miles every day. These walking sessions have become the regimen of my retirement.

I received a letter in the mail from my mortgage company in mid-December of 2010. They were informing me that I only had one more payment and my house would be paid off. I immediately sent them a check before the new year to get the tax deduction. At the same time, I had paid off all of our bills except some of the medical ones. These I would pay off in the next year or two. A friend of mine, Don Denhart, once told me when the right time to retire would be. That time was when you made more money not working, than if you stayed working. How do you know when that is? He said, "you will know." I had not crunched the numbers when I retired but the first thing I noticed was that my pension check was larger than my last school paycheck. This was because I no longer had all the usual deductions. When I turned sixty-two I took my social security and now I definitely made more than working. I also continued to teach driver education. I still loved teaching and working one on one with students is the most rewarding. I worked the after school driving and summer school for seven more years after retirement. That was forty-two more sessions and I watched the pay go up to $25.00 an hour. I didn't need to work, I just enjoyed doing it. With the many investments coming I no longer needed to put myself into "harms" way.

I continued to be a Civil War reenactor and attended many of the 150th anniversary events. Being a participant in these large events is thrilling. Almost like being in the real thing but we aren't shooting any bullets. In 2019 I completed forty years of this hobby and completed another life goal: to reenact longer than I worked my career.

One of the enjoyments of retirement for Connie and me is the chance to do some travelling. When we worked we had to find the time to travel. Now we have the time and can go places in the off season. As of this writing we have made forty trips that lasted three days or more. We have been to Europe four times since 2010 and have taken eight cruises, mostly in the Caribbean. Our 2019 trip to Israel is a highpoint.

I look back and say that I have had a good life. This was a good time to live and I lived in a good place. I am financially set and the decisions I made in the past have helped my situation. I was not born to wealth but now I earn a million dollars every decade that I am retired.

www.ingramcontent.com/pod-product-compliance
Lightning Source LLC
LaVergne TN
LVHW092055060526
838201LV00047B/1396